Library Basics Series

1. *Learn Library of Congress Classification,* Helena Dittmann and Jane Hardy, 2000
2. *Learn Dewey Decimal Classification (Edition 21),* Mary Mortimer, 2000
3. *Learn Descriptive Cataloging,* Mary Mortimer, 2000
4. *Learn LC Subject Access,* Jacki Ganendran, 2000

Learn Library of Congress Classification

Helena Dittmann & Jane Hardy

Library Basics, No.1

The Scarecrow Press, Inc.
Lanham, Maryland, and London
in cooperation with
DocMatrix Pty Ltd, Canberra, Australia
2000

SCARECROW PRESS, INC.

Published in the United States of America
by Scarecrow Press, Inc.
4720 Boston Way, Lanham, Maryland 20706
http://www.scarecrowpress.com

4 Pleydell Gardens, Folkestone
Kent CT20 2DN, England

Design by Andrew Rankine Design Associates pty ltd, Canberra, Australia

British Library and National Library of Australia Cataloguing in Publication
Information Available

Library of Congress Cataloging-in-Publication Data

Dittmann, Helena, 1952-
    Learn Library of Congress classification / Helena Dittmann & Jane Hardy.
        p.   cm.
    Includes bibliographical references and index.
    ISBN 0-8108-3696-3 (alk. paper)
    1. Classification, Library of Congress. I. Hardy, Jane, 1953- . II. Title.
Z696.U4D58   2000
025.4'33—dc21   99-42766
                                             CIP

CONTENTS

PREFACE

This book covers the skills necessary for a classifier using the Library of Congress Classification (LCC) scheme, whether at a professional or paraprofessional level. It is equally suitable for use by library students in universities or colleges, and others who are studying classification by themselves, either with a specific goal or as part of their continuing professional development.

We also envisage that this workbook will be used as a cataloger's reference tool.

You will gain most benefit from this book by working through the chapters in sequence, as each chapter builds on the previous ones.

Not every schedule is used in the workbook. We have selected examples and exercises that portray and reinforce the general principles of LCC which apply across all schedules. You will require access to most schedules, particularly B-BJ, H, L, N, Q, R, S, and T.

LCC schedules are constantly being revised, and the layout and/or instructions in some new editions may differ from those we have used. However the application of the principles and answers to the exercises in this workbook have not changed.

Call numbers are written both vertically and horizontally. Many exercises require that the answers be written vertically. When this is required, there are boxes instead of lines in the answer space.

Throughout the book you will find exercises to practice and test your skills. There are answers for self-checking at the back of the book. You may not always agree completely with the answers given, because there is often room for more than one interpretation or emphasis. It will also depend on your library's classification policies.

This book draws heavily on the experience of the authors and on the use of the Library of Congress Classification in their particular library.

ACKNOWLEDGMENTS

Thanks to Mary Mortimer for her help and encouragement. We wish to acknowledge the assistance of Christine Fulton. Thanks also to our families: Tanya, Dusia, Tim, Alyssa, and Nicholas for their patience and support (no more missed dinners and late nights! Hello weekends and long-lost friends!).

Chapter 1
INTRODUCTION TO CLASSIFICATION

Introduction

Classification is the meaningful grouping of persons, things, animals, and so forth in a systematic way.

Examples in everyday life where systematic groupings are used include:
- supermarkets
- employees
- schools
- mail
- personal papers.

EXERCISE 1.1

Look at the five examples above, where systematic groupings are used, and list some of the ways that you could create order within these examples.

Supermarkets   _____

Employees   _____

Schools   _____

Mail   _____

Personal papers   _____

Library Classification

The basic principle of library classification is to group items on the shelves according to broad fields of knowledge and specific subjects within each field, so that users can find items as easily as possible.

Aims of Library Classification

Library classification schemes:

- order the fields of knowledge in a systematic way
- bring related items together in a helpful sequence
- provide orderly access to the shelves either by browsing or via the catalog
- provide an exact location for an item on the shelves.

Types of Classification

Enumerative classification attempts to spell out (enumerate) all the single and composite subject concepts required:

> e.g., Library of Congress Classification (LCC), Dewey Decimal Classification (DDC) (to a lesser extent).

Synthetic classification, also called faceted classification, lists numbers for single concepts, and allows the classifier to construct (synthesize) numbers for composite subjects:

> e.g., Colon Classification, Universal Decimal Classification, some features of DDC.

Hierarchical classification is based on the division of subjects from the most general to the most specific:

> e.g., DDC, LCC (to a lesser extent).

Features of a Classification Scheme

Library classification schemes generally have the following features:

- schedules
- notation
- index
- number building
- revisions
- tables.

Schedules

The schedules are the printed, enumerated classes, divisions, and so forth of the scheme, arranged in numeric or alphanumeric order. Schedules range from sparse to extremely detailed. In general, the more enumerative the scheme, the more detailed the schedules; the more synthetic, the slimmer the schedules.

The LCC schedules are much lengthier than the DDC schedules, since DDC relies more on number building, whereas LCC lists more of its numbers.

Notation

The notation of a classification scheme is the series of symbols that stand for the classes, subclasses, divisions, and subdivisions of classes.

Notation is used to:
- indicate a subject
- show its relationship to a class
- provide a sequential order for arrangement.

Pure notation is the use of only one type of symbol, such as numbers, e.g., 342.569 in DDC.

Mixed notation is the use of more than one type of symbol, such as numbers and letters, e.g., HM22.F7.G74 1991 in LCC.

Good notation should:
- convey order clearly and automatically
- be as brief and simple as possible
- be easy to say, write, and remember
- be flexible, allowing insertion at any point without dislocating the sequence.

Index
The index is the alphabetical list of the terms used in the schedules, together with the corresponding notation. It should include, as far as possible, all synonyms for the term, and a breakdown of parts of the subject.

There are two types of index:
- specific - with only one entry for each topic mentioned in the schedules
- relative - enumerating all topics and synonyms, and showing the relation of each topic to all the disciplines in which it is found.

Number Building
This is the ability of the scheme to allow the construction of notation to include items not specifically mentioned in the schedules.

Revisions
A classification scheme must be revised frequently, to keep up with new knowledge, new interpretations and new emphases in the presentation of knowledge.

Classification Policy and the User
Classification schemes are often modified by libraries to suit their users' needs. Libraries need a local classification policy that may include decisions such as the following:
- Some equivalent numbers may be used in preference to others.
- Location symbols may be used to group materials—e.g., fiction, reference, periodicals.
- Numbers from copy cataloging records may require adjustment to be a certain length or to fit into a shelflist.
- Libraries may create their own local classification scheme based on an existing scheme, or use another classification scheme for special collections.

For example, some libraries locate their books and journals in separate collections for their users' benefit, and may shelve the journals alphabetically by title.

The Library of Congress assists other libraries by providing alternate classification numbers in its cataloging records for works that can be appropriately classified at another class number. These are usually for incunabula, subject bibliographies, monographs in series, and for works classified by the National Library of Medicine.

EXERCISE 1.2

Use the following questions to revise your understanding of library classification.

a. Give three reasons for classifying a library collection.

b. What is the difference between enumerative and synthetic classification? Give examples.

c. In what order are classification schedules arranged?

d. What is number building? Why is it a desirable feature of a classification scheme?

e. What is hierarchical classification?

f. Why should a library consider the nature of its client group when it classifies its material?

Chapter 2
INTRODUCTION TO LIBRARY OF CONGRESS CLASSIFICATION

Introduction

The Library of Congress Classification was developed for the Library of Congress, beginning in 1897, by James Hanson (chief of the Catalog Department) and his assistant Charles Martel. It was decided that the previous system was no longer adequate for the collection of almost one million volumes. The previous system was Thomas Jefferson's own system for his personal library of nearly 7,000 volumes, which he sold to Congress when it burned down in 1814.

During the development process, several schemes were studied: The Dewey Decimal Classification (in its 5th edition at the time), Cutter's Expansive Classification and the German Halle Schema. None of these systems was adopted in full, but the outline and notation of the main classes are similar to Charles Ammi Cutter's Expansive Classification.

The classification system which they developed was based on the books in the Library of Congress's collection at the time, without any thought that other libraries might want to adopt the system to arrange their own collections.

Each schedule was developed by its own group of subject specialists who based their decisions:
• on the shelf arrangement of the collections as they existed
• on their probable future expansion
• on the special needs of the subject area and how information in the subject area was used.

The schedules were progressively developed over the century. The first schedule, E-F History: America (Western Hemisphere), was published in 1901 and was followed in 1902 by Z Bibliography. Library Science. The first Law schedule—the Law of the United States—appeared in 1969 and other Law schedules are still being produced.

Revisions of schedules used to take many years to complete. Now, the Library of Congress aims to produce two revised editions each year using a new automated system developed at the Library of Congress for this purpose. The system will allow the production of new editions on a regular and frequent basis.

Versions

LCC is available in the following formats:
• *Library of Congress Classification*—printed schedules
• *Classification Plus* (published by the Library of Congress)
• *SuperLCCs*: Gale's LCC schedules combined with *Additions and Changes* (available in print and CD-ROM).

Additional Publications

These publications keep catalogers up-to-date with Library of Congress practices, additions and changes:

- *LC Classification, Additions and Changes* (quarterly publication with the latest additions and changes to all schedules and schedule indexes)
- *Cataloging Service Bulletin* (quarterly update of LCC and shelflisting policies as well as aspects of subject and descriptive cataloging)
- *Subject Cataloging Manual. Shelflisting* (Library of Congress)
- *Subject Cataloging Manual. Classification* (Library of Congress)
- *Library of Congress Subject Headings* (available in print, microfiche, machine-readable and CD-ROM versions).

Additional Sources

Go to the Library of Congress website, http://lcweb.loc.gov, for the following information:

- Library of Congress catalog (access by class number)
- *LC Cataloging Newsline* (online newsletter of the Cataloging Directorate)
- list with the latest publication details for LC classification schedules and manuals
- other links at this site.

Features of LCC
Schedules

The LCC scheme consists of forty-three schedules. Each schedule has:

- a preface
- an outline
- the body of the schedule
- tables after the body
- an index.

Notation

The notation is alphanumeric. A call number:

- starts with one, two, or three letters
- is followed by a number up to four digits
- is sometimes followed by a decimal number
- is followed by an alphanumeric (the cutter number)
- ends with a date of publication.

Index

Each schedule has its own index. There is no one overall index to the scheme.

Hierarchy

The LCC scheme conveys hierarchy through the use of main classes and subclasses and by arrangement of topics from general to specific.

The page layout of the schedules conveys hierarchy and meaning by the order, alignment, and indentation of topics and subtopics, rather than by the numerical values assigned.

Number Building

LCC is an enumerative system, in that it tries to spell out as many subject concepts as possible.

LCC uses number building to expand the classification scheme so that it includes items not already spelled out in the schedules. This is done by using numbers provided in tables in a particular schedule, or by use of the instruction A-Z for alphabetical arrangement by place, person or topic.

Revisions

Schedules are revised individually. They are not all revised at the same time. However, additions and changes are continuous, and the Library of Congress website and various publications of the Library should be consulted for the most recent information.

Advantages of LCC

1. New classes, subclasses, and topics can be added. Not all letters for classes or subclasses have been used, so new ones can be introduced and numbers can be expanded for new topics.
2. LC numbers allow for a unique number to be assigned to a work. This is done by use of cutter numbers, expansion of decimal numbers and the date of publication.
3. Cutter numbers give flexibility so that new topics and geographic areas can be added within a range of numbers.
4. LC numbers are available in Library of Congress Machine Readable Cataloging (MARC) records for copy cataloging purposes and for verifying current LCC practice.
5. The LCC scheme has the resources of a large, nonprofit institution behind it.

Disadvantages of LCC

1. There is a large number of schedules.
2. The scheme has no overall index.
3. The American emphasis in geographical arrangements is a disadvantage for libraries with large international collections and for overseas libraries using the scheme.
4. There is a time lag between revised editions of the schedules. This is becoming less true with the automation of the schedules.
5. Changes in the schedules need to be checked in supplementary publications (also less of a problem due to automation).
6. New editions of the schedules sometimes require reclassification decisions—e.g., JX has been replaced by the subclasses JZ (International relations) and KZ (Law of nations).
7. There is little documentation on how to use the classification. The publication of the Library of Congress's policies on classification and shelflisting have filled this gap to some extent.
8. The classification depends on acquisitions of the Library of Congress. The subject coverage of the collection is comprehensive, but not exhaustive.

Classifying with LCC

Classifying with LCC involves several steps. This workbook will cover all of the following:

1. Examine the work in hand to determine the subject.

2. Look at subject headings.

3. Write down keywords that represent the subject.

4. Choose the relevant schedule.

5. Use the index in that schedule as your starting point.

6. Look in the body of the schedule and select your number.

7. Assign a cutter number for the main entry.

8. Add the date of publication.

9. Check the shelflist and adjust if necessary.

10. The item is ready for labelling and for shelving.

Determining the Subject (Steps 1-3)

The classifier must examine the work in hand. This examination includes:

- title - may or may not be helpful
- other title - often more useful
- table of contents - good indicator of the main topics
- foreword, preface, introduction - usually state the author's intention and subject coverage
- book cover - may give information about author and summary of content
- text - use to confirm your ideas about the subject.

It is very useful to look at the subject headings in the bibliographic record or Cataloging-in-Publication (CIP) entry to determine subject content. Captions in the schedules are sometimes the same as Library of Congress Subject Headings (LCSH), which will assist you in using the index of a schedule.

LCSH gives class numbers for many headings.

Principles of Classifying with LCC

1. Classify works according to their subject matter.
2. Use the most specific number available.
3. Give each work a unique number.
4. Classify a work where it will be most useful to the user.
5. Classify a work which covers two or more subjects:
   - with the one that receives fuller treatment
   - at a broader class, if that class includes all the subjects as subclasses.

Call Numbers

A call number is the number on the spine label of a library item, which shows where it is shelved. It usually consists of a class number, a book number and often a location symbol. For example:

folio   location symbol
NA   } class number
7105 }

.D58 } book number (includes date of publication)
1997 }

The location symbol shows where the item is housed. The class number indicates the subject. The book number relates to the item itself.

The call number can also be written in the following ways:

NA7105   LC929.3.T5.B35 1982   QA
.D58   76
1997   .7
                                                 .S36
                                                 1994

In CIP entries, the call number may appear without the decimal point before the book number:

PS3525.E6645A6 1997

In MARC records, the call number may appear in the same way as above without a decimal point but separated by a delimiter. For example:

CAL |ab |PS3525.E6645|A6 1997

Some libraries use other ways of formatting call numbers.

EXERCISE 2.1

Use the following questions to revise your understanding of LCC.

a.   Why was LCC developed?

b.   The LCC schedules do not have an index. Comment on this statement.

c.   What does alphanumeric notation mean?

d.   What do you need to determine before you can start to classify?

e.   How many schedules are there?

f.   In the following examples, write each call number in a different way.

1.   NA7105
     .D58
     1997

2.   PS3525.E6645A6 1997

3.   LC929.3.T5.B35 1982

Chapter 3
STRUCTURE OF LIBRARY OF CONGRESS CLASSIFICATION

Main Classes

The main classes are expressed as alphabetics. The letters I, O, W, X, Y have not been assigned subject areas, but could be used for future expansion.

A	General
B	Philosophy. Psychology. Religion
C-F	History
G	Geography. Anthropology. Leisure
H	Social Sciences
J	Political Science
K	Law
L	Education
M	Music
N	Fine Arts
P	Language and Literature
Q	Science
R	Medicine
S	Agriculture. Landscape Architecture
T	Technology
U	Military Science
V	Naval Science
Z	Bibliography. Publishing. Librarianship

EXERCISE 3.1

Refer to the list of main classes on the previous page, and write down the letters which represent the following classes.

a. Military science

_____

b. Religion

_____

c. Science

_____

d. Education

_____

e. Law

_____

f. Librarianship

_____

g. Geography

_____

EXERCISE 3.2

Identify the subject of each work and write down the letter of the main class to which it belongs.

a. Wartime submarines

_____

b. Encyclopaedia Britannica

_____

c. Public libraries

_____

d. Treatment of cancer

_____

e. Landscape painting

_____

f. Astronomy for beginners

_____

g. Growing orchids

_____

h. Teaching adults

_____

i. Defense in the modern world

_____

j. History of jazz

_____

k. Designing buildings

_____

l. Federal government administration

_____

m. Voyages of Christopher Columbus

_____

n. The American legal system

_____

o. Bridge engineering   _____

p. Biblical studies   _____

q. The Japanese economy   _____

r. The plays of William Shakespeare   _____

s. The American Civil War   _____

Subclasses

The main classes of LCC have subclasses. For example, the subclasses of the main class H are:

H	Social Sciences (General)
HA	Statistics
HB	Economic Theory. Demography
HC	Economic History and Conditions
HD	Economic History and Conditions
HE	Transportation and Communications
HF	Commerce
HG	Finance
HJ	Public Finance
HM	Sociology (General)
HN	Social History and Conditions. Social problems. Social Reform
HQ	The Family. Marriage. Woman
HS	Societies: Secret, Benevolent, etc.
HT	Communities. Classes. Races
HV	Social Pathology. Social and Public Welfare. Criminology
HX	Socialism. Communism. Anarchism

EXERCISE 3.3

Refer to the list of subclasses for H and identify the subclasses to which the following subjects belong.

a. Secret societies

    _____

b. Communism

    _____

c. Statistics

    _____

d. Marriage

    _____

e. Transport

    _____

EXERCISE 3.4

Using the list of subclasses for H, write down the subclass to which each of the following topics belongs.

a. World banking

    _____

b. Violence in the home

    _____

c. The future of speed rail

    _____

d. Encyclopedia of sociology

    _____

e. Readings on international trade

    _____

f. Statistical dictionary

    _____

g. The caste system in India

    _____

h. Government income and expenditure

    _____

i. Social science methodology

    _____

j. Origins of the Boy Scout movement

    _____

k. Population projections for the year 2000

    _____

l. Development of social movements in Canada

    _____

m. Sociology of crime

    _____

n. Readings in Marxist philosophy

    _____

o. The American economy

    _____

p. Origins of modern social theory

    _____

The Schedules

There are forty-three individual classification schedules (at the time of publication) for the main classes and subclasses of LCC. The tables for the P-PZ and K classes are published separately.

The list of schedules includes the date of publication in parentheses.

A	General works. 5th ed. (1998)
B-BJ	Philosophy. Psychology. 1996 ed. (1996)
BL, BM, BP, BQ	Religion: Religions. Hinduism, Judaism, Islam, Buddhism. 3rd ed. (1984)
BR-BV	Religion: Christianity, Bible (1987)
BX	Religion: Christian denominations (1985)
C	Auxiliary Sciences of History (1996)
D-DJ	History (General), History of Europe. Part 1. 3rd ed. (1990)
DJK-DK	History of Eastern Europe: General, Soviet Union, Poland (1987)
DL-DR	History of Europe. Part 2. 3rd ed. (1990)
DS-DX	History of Asia, Africa, Australia, New Zealand, etc. (1998)
E-F	History: America (1995)
G	Geography. Maps. Anthropology. Recreation. 4th ed. (1976)
H	Social Sciences (1997)
J	Political Science (1997)
K	Law (General). 1998 ed. (1999)
K	K tables: form division tables for Law. 1999 ed. (1999)
KD	Law of the United Kingdom and Ireland (1998)
KDZ, KG-KH	Law of the Americas, Latin America, West Indies (1984)
KE	Law of Canada. 1999 ed. (1999)
KF	Law of the United States. Preliminary ed. (1969)
KJ-KKZ	Law of Europe (1989)
KJV-KJW	Law of France. 1999 ed. (1999)

KK-KKC	Law of Germany (1982)
KL-KWZ	Law of Asia and Eurasia, Africa, Pacific area and Antarctica (1993)
KZ	Law of Nations (1998)
L	Education. 1998 ed. (1999)
M	Music and books on music. 1998 ed. (1999)
N	Fine Arts (1996)
P-PA	Philology and linguistics (General). Greek language and literature. Latin language and literature (1997)
P-PZ	Language and literature tables. 1998 ed. (1998)
PB-PH	Modern European languages. 1999 ed. (1999)
PG	Russian literature (1948)
PJ-PK	Oriental philology and literature, Indo-Iranian philology and literature. 2nd ed. (1988)
PL-PM	Languages of Eastern Asia, Africa, Oceania; Hyperborean, Indian, and artificial languages. 2nd ed. (1988)
P-PM	Supplement: Index to languages and dialects. 4th ed. (1991)
PN	Literature (General) (1997)
PR, PS, PZ	English and American literature, Juvenile Belles Lettres. 1998 ed. (1999)
PQ	French, Italian, Spanish and Portuguese literatures (1998)
PT (Part 1)	German literature (1989)
PT (Part 2)	Dutch and Scandinavian literatures. 2nd ed. (1992)
Q	Science (1996)
R	Medicine (1995)
S	Agriculture (1996)
T	Technology (1995)
U-V	Military Science. Naval Science (1996)
Z	Bibliography and Library Science (1995)

EXERCISE 3.5

List the history schedules.

Class	Title

EXERCISE 3.6

Refer to the list of schedules. Which schedule would you use to find an LC number for the following?

a.   A book of Russian poetry   _____

b.   A history of Australia   _____

c.   Manual of geology   _____

d.   Henry Moore's sculpture   _____

e.   Guide to camping   _____

f.   Canadian law   _____

g.   Pediatrics   _____

h.   Woodwind instruments   _____

Physical Format of the Schedules

Each schedule has the following components:

- preface
- contents page
- outline of the schedule
- main body of the schedule
- tables
- index.

Preface

The preface gives the history of the schedule, the changes from previous editions and the reasons for those changes.

Contents Page

The contents page lists the outline, subclasses, tables and index for the schedule. Here is an example from the R schedule.

	Out-line
MEDICINE (General)	R
PUBLIC ASPECTS OF MEDICINE	RA
PATHOLOGY	RB
INTERNAL MEDICINE	RC
SURGERY	RD
OPHTHALMOLOGY	RE
OTORHINOLARYNGOLOGY	RF
GYNECOLOGY AND OBSTETRICS	RG
PEDIATRICS	RJ
DENTISTRY	RK
DERMATOLOGY	RL
THERAPEUTICS. PHARMACOLOGY	RM
PHARMACY AND MATERIA MEDICA	RS
NURSING	RT
BOTANIC, THOMSONIAN, AND ECLECTIC MEDICINE	RV
HOMEOPATHY	RX
OTHER SYSTEMS OF MEDICINE	RZ
R1 MEDICAL EDUCATION AND SCHOOLS	Table
	Index

Outline

The outline provides a detailed summary of the topics and subtopics in the schedule.

It is useful because it gives an overall picture of how the topics are arranged within the schedule, and can help you to decide which part of the schedule to go to for a class number.

OUTLINE

RG	1-991	Gynecology and obstetrics
	104-104.7	Operative gynecology
	133-137.6	Conception. Artificial insemination. Contraception
	138	Sterilization of women
	159-208	Functional and systemic disorders. Endocrine gynecology
	211-483	Abnormalities and diseases of the female genital organs
	484-485	Urogynecology and obstetric urology. Urogynecologic surgery
	491-499	Diseases of the breast
	500-991	Obstetrics
	551-591	Pregnancy
	600-650	The embryo and fetus
	648	Spontaneous abortion. Miscarriage
	651-721	Labor. Parturition
	725-791	Obstetric operations. Operative obstetrics
	801-871	Puerperal state
	940-991	Maternal care. Prenatal care services
RJ	1-570	Pediatrics
	47.3-47.4	Genetic aspects
	50-51	Examination. Diagnosis
	52-53	Therapeutics
	59-60	Infant and neonatal morbidity and mortality
	91	Supposed prenatal influence. Prenatal culture. Stirpiculture
	101-103	Child health. Child health services
	125-145	Physiology of children and adolescents
	206-235	Nutrition and feeding of children and adolescents
	240	Immunization of children (General)
	242-243	Hospital care
	245-247	Nursing of children. Pediatric nursing
	250-250.3	Premature infants
	251-325	Newborn infants Including physiology, care, treatment, diseases
	370-550	Diseases of children and adolescents
	499-507	Mental disorders. Child psychiatry

The Body of the Schedule

Each of the schedules has been developed by a separate group of subject specialists, so the arrangement and wording vary, as do some of the captions (i.e., headings and subheadings), depending on what is appropriate to a subject area.

There is a basic pattern to the arrangement of works within each class, subclass or subject area.

The arrangement is a progression from the general to the specific as follows:
- periodicals and other works based on form, such as:
    - society publications
    - collections
    - dictionaries or encyclopedias
    - conference, exhibition, or museum publications
    - yearbooks
    - directories
    - documents
- theory, philosophy
- history, biography
- general works
- law
- study and teaching, research
- subjects and more specific topics within those subjects.

Indentation of captions is used throughout the schedules, and is important in showing the hierarchical relationships of topics. The use of indentation is covered in detail later in this chapter.

Look at the arrangement in the following example, Ecology, in the QH subclass. It includes some of the elements from the above list, but has additional captions that are specific to this subject area, e.g.,

Nomenclature, terminology, notation, abbreviations
Classification

QH	BIOLOGY (GENERAL)	QH

Ecology
   Class here works on general ecology and general animal
      ecology. For works on ecology of individual animals
      and groups of animals, see the animal
   Cf. HX550.E25, Communism and ecology
   Cf. QH546, Ecological genetics
   For ecology of a particular topographic area, see
      QH101+
   For human ecology, see GF1+
   For plant ecology, see QK900+

540	Periodicals, societies, congresses, serial collections, yearbooks
540.3	Collected works (nonserial)
540.4	Dictionaries and encyclopedias
540.5	Philosophy
540.6	Nomenclature, terminology, notation, abbreviations
540.7	Classification
	History
540.8	General works
540.83.A-Z	By region or country, A-Z
541	General works, treatises, and textbooks
541.13	Popular works
541.14	Juvenile works
541.142	Handbooks, tables, formulas, etc.
541.145	Addresses, essays, lectures
541.15.A-Z	Special aspects of the subject as a whole, A-Z
541.15.A9	Autoradiographic techniques
541.15.B54	Biological assay
541.15.B56	Biological diversity

   For local, see QH84.1-QH198
   Cf. QH75+, Biological diversity
   Cf. QH541.15.S64, Species diversity

541.15.C44	Chemical ecology
541.15.C55	Closed ecological systems
541.15.C67	Corridors
541.15.D6	Documentation
541.15.E24	Ecological heterogeneity
541.15.E25	Economic ecology
541.15.E26	Ecophysiology

   Cf. QK905, Plant ecophysiology
   Cf. QP82+, Animal ecophysiology

541.15.E27	Ecotones
541.15.E45	Electronic data processing
	Heterogeneity, Ecological, see QH541.15.E24
541.15.I5	Indicators (Biology)
541.15.L35	Landscape ecology
541.15.M3	Mathematical models
541.15.M34	Mathematics
541.15.M63	Molecular ecology
541.15.M64	Monitoring
541.15.N84	Null models
541.15.R34	Radioactive tracers
541.15.R4	Remote sensing

EXERCISE 3.7

From our excerpt from QH540 Ecology, write the caption at the following numbers.

a. QH540

_____

b. QH540.4

_____

c. QH540.8

_____

d. QH541

_____

e. QH541.15.A-Z

_____

f. QH541.15.E25

_____

EXERCISE 3.8

From the same example, provide the subclass and number for the following topics.

a. An ecology journal

_____

b. Philosophy of ecology

_____

c. A general work on the history of ecology

_____

d. General textbooks on ecology

_____

e. Tables and formulas for ecologists

_____

f. A book on chemical ecology

_____

g. A book on landscape ecology

_____

Indentation

Indentation is very important in the page layout of the LCC schedules. It shows the hierarchy within topics and subtopics.

Indentation at the top of pages also serves to put the topics on the page in context. It summarizes the hierarchy, from general to specific, developed over previous pages.

Here is an example of indentation at the top of a page:

E	UNITED STATES	E
	The Civil War, 1861-1865	
	Armies. Troops	
	The Union Army	
	By state	
	District of Columbia	
	Military organizations -- Continued	
501.7	Artillery, Heavy	
	For the seceded states, this subdivision	
	is used for Union troops	
	Subarranged by number or name of regiment,	
	A-Z, and by author, A-Z	
501.8	Artillery, Light	
	For the seceded states, this subdivision	
	is used for Union troops	
	Subarranged by number or name of regiment,	
	A-Z, and by author, A-Z	

The excerpt at CR from the C schedule illustrates the importance of reading the page and following the indentation. You may need a ruler to read pages and to select the correct number.

	Royalty. Insignia. Regalia, crown and coronets, etc.
	Class here general works only
	Cf. NK7400+, Decorative art
	For heraldry aspects, see CR53
	For royalty of a particular country, see CR199+
4480	General works
4485.A-Z	Special, A-Z
4485.C7	Crown
4485.O7	Orb
4485.T5	Throne
	Chivalry and knighthood (Orders, decorations, etc.)
4501	Museums. Collections
4505	Dictionaries. Encyclopedias
	History
4509	General works
	By period
4511	Early
4513	Medieval
4515	Modern
4519	Philosophy. Theory. Relation to other topics
4529.A-Z	By region or country, A-Z
	General works
4531	Through 1800
4533	1801-
4534	General special

The two main topic areas in the excerpt above are:

> Royalty. Insignia. Regalia, crown and coronets, etc.
> Chivalry and knighthood (Orders, decorations, etc.)

Each has a list of indented captions. For example:
- A general work on Royal insignia is classified at CR4480.
- A general work on the history of Chivalry and knighthood is at CR4509.
- However, general works on Chivalry and knighthood are at CR4531+.

Exercise 3.9

Look at the CR excerpt and indicate the number that you would assign to this topic.

a. A general work on the history of knighthood

    _____

b. A historical work on knights and knighthood in medieval times

    _____

c. A book about crowns

    _____

d. A dictionary of orders and decorations

    _____

e. A general work about the use of ceremonial regalia

    _____

Notes

Notes may accompany LC class numbers and headings. They can indicate the scope of that number, or may refer the classifier to another number or section of the schedule.

Scope notes explain the type of works to be classified at that subject, and may refer the classifier to related topics elsewhere in the schedule or in another schedule.

For example, at QH540:

> Ecology
>   Class here works on general ecology and general animal ecology.

Including notes list topics which are included within a subject.

For example, at Animal Culture SF101:

> Brands and branding, and other means of identifying
>   Including cattle brands and earmarks

See notes refer the classifier to a number elsewhere in the schedules, often as a result of a reclassification decision.

For example, at QH540:

> For ecology of a particular topographic area, see QH101+
> For human ecology, see GF1+
> For plant ecology, see QK900+

A number in parentheses indicates that the number is no longer in use, and a see reference is given.

For example, at TH6518 Plumbing and pipefitting:

(6525) Rural domestic water supply	
see TD927	

Law. Legislation: This caption appears less frequently in the schedules with the completion of the K schedules.

For example, at TR 193-195 Photography:

(193-195) Law. Legislation	
see class K	

Confer (Cf.) notes indicate that related topics are classified elsewhere in the schedules.

For example, at QH540:

Cf. HX550.E25, Communism and ecology	
Cf. QH546, Ecological genetics	

Apply table at notes refer you to a table with subdivision instructions, so that the same instruction is not repeated on the same page or several times over a couple of pages.

For example, at NK3650.5.A-Z:

By region or country, A-Z	
Apply table at NK3649.35.A-Z	

Another example at BJ351-982 shows a more extensive use of this type of note. The instruction "Apply table at BJ351-982" is used repeatedly over two pages.

Other notes are used in the schedules, most of which are self-explanatory. This book does not treat notes used in earlier editions of schedules.

EXERCISE 3.10

Go to SB118.48 and find examples of the following types of notes.

a. Two examples of "Cf." (confer) notes

_____

_____

b. Four examples of "see" notes

_____

_____

_____

_____

c. One example of "Apply table at" notes

_____

d. Three examples of "Including" notes

_____

_____

_____

Tables

All schedules have tables. Chapter 5 deals with different types of tables.

Some tables are within the body of the schedule and apply to the class number under which they occur.

For example, at TR640 from the T schedule:

	Artistic photography
640	Periodicals, societies, congresses, etc.
642	General works
	Exhibitions
	Prefer TR650 TR654 for collections of photographs
	Works of more than one photographer
	United States
644	General works
645.A-Z	By city, A-Z
	Under each city:
	.x *General works*
	.x2A-.x2Z *By museum, A-Z*
646.A-Z	Other regions or countries, A-Z
	Under each country:
	.x *General works*
	.x2A-.x2Z *By city, A-Z*

Other tables apply across an entire class or subclass, and are found at the back of the schedule before the index.

For example, Table H16 from the H schedule:

H16	TABLE OF ECONOMIC SUBDIVISIONS (5 NOS.)	H16
	Documents	
1.A1-A3	Serial documents	
1.A4-A42	Separate documents	
1.A5-Z	Periodicals. Societies. Serials	
	Biography	
	For particular industries, see HD	
1.5.A2	Collective	
1.5.A3-Z	Individual, A-Z	
2	General works	
2.5	Natural resources	
3.A-Z	Local, A-Z	
	Used under countries only	
4	Colonies	
	Including exploitation and economic conditions.	
	For colonial administration and policy, see JV.	
5.A-Z	Special topics (not otherwise provided for), A-Z	
	For list of topics, see HC79	
	For special topics in areas within a country, see subdivision 3, Local	

Index

There is a detailed index in the back of each schedule, and the entries refer you to a specific LC number in that schedule. The index is often the first place to go to when assigning an LC number.

Note: There is no one index to the LCC schedules. Each schedule has its own index.

This is an excerpt from the index in the R schedule. The entries in the index refer you to the class number in the schedule.

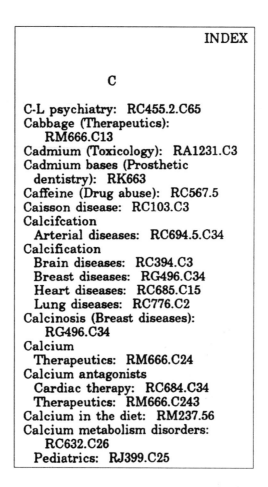

EXERCISE 3.11

Refer to the indexes in the R and N schedules. When required, go to the class number in the schedule.

a.   What is the class number for movable kidney in the index?

b.   Find the entry for artificial kidneys in the index and write down the class number.

c.   Find another entry for artificial kidneys in the index. What is it?

d.   What is the caption in the schedule at the class number for multiple birth?

e.   What is the class number for comic book illustration?

f.   What is the caption in the schedule for computer art?

g.   What is the first caption in the schedule under Sculpture?

h.   Is there an entry in the index for doodling?

i.   Is there an entry in the index for graffiti?

EXERCISE 3.12

Assign a class number from the schedules for the following topics and subjects.

- Decide what the subject is.
- Decide which schedule it belongs to.
- Use the index in the schedule to help you find the class number. Otherwise use the contents page and the outline.

		Schedule	Class Number
a.	Cancer research	_____	_____
b.	Japanese gardens	_____	_____
c.	General work on forest fires	_____	_____
d.	A bibliography of bookbinding	_____	_____
e.	Clay pot cookery	_____	_____
f.	An accounting dictionary	_____	_____
g.	Breeding Siberian huskies	_____	_____
h.	Keynesian economics	_____	_____
i.	Making Christmas decorations	_____	_____
j.	History of osteopathy	_____	_____
k.	Preserving cherries	_____	_____
l.	Nursing in Australia	_____	_____
m.	Women landscape architects	_____	_____
n.	History of geometry	_____	_____
o.	The OCLC library network	_____	_____
p.	Manual for a Yashica camera	_____	_____
q.	Bonsai gardens	_____	_____
r.	The solar system for children	_____	_____
s.	The adventures of Charles Darwin, the naturalist	_____	_____

Chapter 4
BUILDING A CALL NUMBER

Call Numbers

Call numbers in LCC are alphanumeric—that is, they have a mixed notation of letters and numbers.

Call numbers are made up of two main parts—the class number and the book number.

The class number may consist of:
- the class or subclass letters (one to three letters)
- a whole number which subdivides that class or subclass
- decimal extension (according to the schedules)
- cutter number (according to the schedules).

} *groups related materials together*

The book number consists of:
- cutter number for the main entry
- year of publication.

} *uniquely identifies different works in the same class*

Example 1

Here is a simple call number for an introductory text on geometry by Andrew Brady published in 1998:

QA
445
.B73
1998

QA	represents the subclass Mathematics from the Q schedule
445	subdivides Mathematics more specifically to Geometry
.B73	is the cutter number based on the main entry of the bibliographic record (which could be a personal author, corporate author or the title of a work)
	In this call number the main entry is the author. The cutter number: - is preceded by a decimal point - is constructed using the Library of Congress Cutter Table
1998	is the date of publication

Example 2

This example, a book on computer programming languages by Schmidt and published in 1994, has an additional line with a decimal extension:

QA
76
.7
.S36
1994

QA	Mathematics
76	Electronic computers
.7	Programming languages The decimal extension breaks down the subject of computers to a more specific topic.
.S36	Cutter for the author in the main entry (Schmidt)
1994	Year of publication

Example 3

This is a book titled *Reengineering COBOL* by Levey, published in 1995.

The call number follows the same pattern, with an additional cutter number representing a specific programming language:

QA
76
.73
.C25
.L48
1995

QA	Mathematics
76	Electronic computers
.73	Individual programming languages
.C25	First cutter for the programming language COBOL
.L48	Second cutter for the author in the main entry (Levey)
1995	Year of publication

The following excerpt from the Q schedule shows the breakdown of the topic Programming languages within the broader subject area of Computers.

QA	MATHEMATICS	QA
	Instruments and machines	
	Calculating machines	
	Electronic computers. Computer science	
	Digital computers – Continued	
76.5	General works	
76.52	Juvenile works	
76.525	Microcomputer workstations	
76.53	Time-sharing data processing	
	Real-time data processing	
76.54	General works	
76.545	Transaction systems	
	Online data processing	
	Including general online information services and general videotex systems	
76.55	General works	
76.57.A-Z	Special systems, A-Z	
76.57.A43	America Online	
76.57.C65	CompuServe	
76.57.D44	DELPHI	
76.57.E88	eWorld (Online service)	
76.57.G45	GEnie (Videotex system)	
76.57.M52	Microsoft Network	
76.57.M55	Minitel	
76.57.P75	Prodigy (Online service)	
76.57.S68	SOURCE (Videotex system)	
76.57.T44	TÉLÉTEL (Videotex system)	
76.57.U43	UMI Online (Videotex system)	
76.575	Multimedia systems	
	Cf. QA76.76.I59, Interactive multimedia	
76.58	Parallel processing. Parallel computers	
76.59	Mobile computing	
	Programming	
	For computer programs and other software, see QA76.75+	
76.6	General works	
76.612	Constraint programming	
76.615	Declarative programming	
76.618	Evolutionary programming	
76.62	Functional programming	
76.63	Logic programming	
76.635	Microprogramming	
76.64	Object-oriented programming	
76.642	Parallel programming	
76.65	Visual programming	
76.66	Systems programming	
	Programming languages	
76.7	General works	
76.73.A-Z	Individual languages, A-Z	
	e.g.	
76.73.A24	ALGOL	
76.73.A27	APL	
76.73.B3	BASIC	
76.73.C25	COBOL	

EXERCISE 4.1

Look at Examples 2 and 3 above and the excerpt from the QA Mathematics page of the schedules. Highlight the number and caption for each example.

EXERCISE 4.2

Using the excerpt from QA Mathematics:

a.   Name the subclass

b.   What is the class number for a general work on digital computers?

c.   What number would you choose for a work about the DELPHI online data processing system?

d.   What is the class number for general works on programming?

e.   What is the class number for the programming language BASIC?

EXERCISE 4.3

1.	2.	3.	4.	5.
E 462 .O28 1998	F 73 .18 .H58 1995	ND 1489 .C65 1997	SF 515 .5 .S64 .M33 1991	PN 1992 .7 .B75 1995

a.   Identify the class number for each of the above call numbers.

1.

2.

3.

4.

5.

b. Which of the examples has a decimal extension?

c. Identify the main entry cutter in each of the above call numbers.

1.

2.

3.

4.

5.

d. What is the book number for each of the call numbers?

1.

2.

3.

4.

5.

Exercise 4.4

Using the schedules, identify the correct schedule and find the class number for the following titles.

a. The perfect tense in Latin grammar

         _____

b. General principles for research in computational linguistics

         _____

c. Plato on good and evil

         _____

d. Philosophical history of twentieth-century psychology

         _____

e. The influence and effects of mass media on youth

         _____

f. The Great Depression of 1929: a study of an economic crisis

         _____

g. The Washington Cycling Club, Chicago

         _____

h. The official report of the Games of the XXIIIrd Olympiad, Los Angeles, 1984

         _____

i. Icelandic civilization

         _____

j. A historical biography of women in Bulgaria

         _____

Cutter Numbers

Cutter numbers are used to order materials alphabetically on the shelf within a class, subclass or subject area.

The term "cutter number" is derived from the name of Charles Ammi Cutter, who conceived the idea of using alphanumeric symbols as a method of arranging books in alphabetical order within a given class.

Cutter devised a two-figure author table which was later expanded by Kate Sanborn, and published in 1969 as the *Cutter-Sanborn Three-Figure Author Table*.

The Library of Congress has modified Cutter's table to serve the special needs of its collections.

The Library of Congress Cutter Table is used in this book to form cutter numbers.

Cutter numbers are used in different ways:
- to give a unique call number, based on the main entry of a work
- to indicate the specific title of a given work
- to indicate the geographical area covered by a work
- to indicate a special topic covered by a work
- to shelve certain works at a given class number before or after others.

A cutter number:
- begins with the first letter of a word
- is followed by a decimal number derived from the second and subsequent letters of that word
- is always preceded by a decimal point
- is formed using a table.

Cutter Table

(1) After initial vowels

for the second letter:	b	d	l-m	n	p	r	s-t	u-y
use number:	2	3	4	5	6	7	8	9

(2) After initial letter S

for the second letter:	a	ch	e	h-i	m-p	t	u	w-z
use number:	2	3	4	5	6	7	8	9

(3) After initial letters Qu

for the second letter:	a	e	i	o	r	t	y
use number:	3	4	5	6	7	8	9

For initial letters Qa-Qt, use: 2-29

(4) After other initial consonants

for the second letter:	a	e	i	o	r	u	y
use number:	3	4	5	6	7	8	9

(5) For expansion

for the letter:	a-d	e-h	i-l	m-o	p-s	t-v	w-z
use number:	3	4	5	6	7	8	9

Using the LC Cutter Table

Study the table. Note the breakdown into five paragraphs:

- Paragraph (1) is for words beginning with a vowel—a, e, i, o, u.
- Paragraph (2) is used for words beginning with the letter S.
- Paragraph (3) is used for words beginning with the letters Qu.
- Paragraph (4) is used for words beginning with all other consonants.
- Paragraph (5) is used for the second digit of the cutter number.

Example 1

Cumming is the surname of an author.

The cutter number is based on the first three letters of the name, **Cum**ming.

The first letter points you to the paragraph in the Cutter Table which determines the first digit:
- The letter **C** points you to paragraph (4)

The second letter is used to find the value of the first digit:
- The value for the letter **u** in paragraph (4) is **8**

The third letter is used to find the value of the second digit:
- The value for the letter **m** in paragraph (5) is **6**

C	becomes		.C
u	becomes	8 paragraph (4)	.C8
m	becomes	6 paragraph (5)	.C86

Example 2

The cutter number is based on a title. The title is *Artist's manual.*

The cutter number is based on the first three letters of the first word in the title, **Art**ist's. The first letter is a vowel, so paragraph (1) is the starting point.

A	becomes		.A
r	becomes	7 paragraph (1)	.A7
t	becomes	8 paragraph (5)	.A78

In these two examples, the cutter numbers conform exactly to the Cutter Table. However, in many cases, the cutter number will need to be adjusted to fit into your shelflist. The shelflist will be discussed later in this chapter.

Note that:
- not all letters appear in the table. When the letter you have is not listed, choose the letter and corresponding number nearest your letter. You may choose the lower or higher number. The final cutter number will be decided when you check your shelflist.

  For example, for the name Nguyen:
  - in paragraph (4), the letter "g" is exactly between the letters "e" and "i"
  - you could choose either .N48 or .N58
  - check your shelflist to decide the final number.

- the digits 1 and 0 (zero) are not used in the table. Library of Congress practice is never to end a cutter number with 1 or 0, as it can result in an unnecessarily long decimal extension.

EXERCISE 4.5

Using the LC Cutter Table, create cutter numbers for the following authors.

a. Appiah _____

b. Brettell _____

c. O'Reilly _____

d. Cousineau _____

e. Schonell _____

f. Takagi _____

g. Dasgupta _____

h. D'Ambrosio _____

i. Rubin _____

j. Wang _____

k. Dukic _____

l. Sanchez _____

m. Quinlan _____

n. Papadopoulos _____

o. Isfahani _____

p.   Beauchamps

q.   Somare

r.   Urquhart

s.   Fagyas

t.   Tippet

u.   Halupka

v.   Li

w.   Smith

EXERCISE 4.6

Create cutter numbers for the following titles.

a.   Leaders and managers

b.   Between the earthquakes

c.   Qualitative evaluation methods

d.   Emergence of a free press

e.   Out of Africa

f.   Social anthropology

g.   Interviewing skills

h.   Quince novelas hispanoamericanas

i.   Sept ans chez les hommes libres

j.   Education and political development

k.   Principles and practices of identifying infectious diseases

l.   Composing an opera

m.   Industrialization and culture

n.   Algebraic theory of semigroups

o.   Undersea lightwave communications

p.   Jurassic Park

EXERCISE 4.7

Create cutter numbers for the following corporate authors.

a. World Bank _____

b. Universal Studios _____

c. British Broadcasting Corporation _____

d. Mambo (Firm) _____

e. United States. Congress. Committee on Armed Services _____

f. Qantas Airways _____

Cuttering and the LC Filing Rules

The Library of Congress follows the *Library of Congress Filing Rules* for arranging entries in its catalogs, LCC and the shelflist. This workbook follows these filing rules when creating cutter numbers.

Individual libraries may have different policies on these filing rules and this will affect how you cutter.

Here are some general points to guide you in assigning cutter numbers:

Rule	Example
Ignore initial articles in titles such as the, a, an (and articles in other languages e.g., le, das, los, il, l')	The sea [title main entry] - cutter as .S
Do not ignore initial articles and prefixes in personal and place names	El Paso [place name] - cutter as .E46 (first digit for L, second digit for P)
Ignore hyphens	On-line - cutter as .O55 (first digit for N, second digit for L)
Treat abbreviations as written (do not spell out)	St. Nicholas - cutter as .S76 (first digit for T, second digit for N)
Mac and Mc—(do not treat as the same and do not spell out Mc)	Macdonald - cutter as .M33 McDonald - cutter as .M43

EXERCISE 4.8

Create cutter numbers for the following.

a.   El Greco _____

b.   St. Augustine _____

c.   MacIntosh _____

d.   Dal Santo _____

e.   McManus _____

f.   Saint Agnes _____

g.   Le Mesurier _____

h.   An acoustic experience _____

i.   De Souza _____

j.   Los jardines de Granada _____

k.   McKenzie-Clay _____

Date of Publication in Call Numbers

The Library of Congress began the practice of adding the date of imprint or copyright to a call number in 1982.

For most works, the date in the "publication, distribution" field (MARC tag 260) of the bibliographic record is the source of the date in the call number.

The following table lists the recommended date for the call number. This table and other shelflisting policies and procedures can be found in the Library of Congress *Subject Cataloging Manual. Shelflisting.*

Date in Bibliographic Record	Date in Call Number
1976?	1976
ca. 1976	1976
1981, c1980	1981
1971, c1972	1972
1979 [i.e., 1978]	1978
1962 or 1963	1962
1969 (1973 printing)	1969
1980 printing, c1957	1957
1979 [distributed] 1980	1979
1979-1981	1979
between 1977 and 1980	1977
1978/79 [i.e., 1978 or 1979]	1978
1977 (cover 1978)	1978
197-	1970z (if corporate body, use 1970)
197-?	1970z (if corporate body, use 1970)
19--	1900z (if corporate body, use 1900)
19--?	1900z (if corporate body, use 1900)

Note that the letter "z" is used to represent an unknown date.

Other Situations

- Congresses or conferences—use the date of the congress or conference and not the date of publication.

- The Library of Congress also uses work letters after the date in the call number. Consult the Library of Congress *Subject Cataloging Manual. Shelflisting* for more details and examples. Work letters are used:
  - To distinguish between different editions of a work with the same date in the imprint:
    - .P44 1983   New York : Viking Press, 1983
    - .P44 1983b   London : Chatto and Windus, 1983
    - .P44 1983c   New York : McGraw-Hill, 1983

  - For facsimile editions:
    - .G78 1960
    - .G78 1960a
    - .G78 1960aa

  - For works on the same topic published in the same year with the same corporate author as the main entry, letters start with "a" and continue through the alphabet in order of receipt:
    - .R37 1990
    - .R37 1990a
    - .R37 1990b

EXERCISE 4.9

Write down the date you would assign to a call number from each of the publication statements in the following list. Refer to the table of dates above.

a. New York : Crowell, 1991 [i.e., 1993]

_____

b. Tokyo : Zokeisha Publications, 1990 (1992 printing)

_____

c. London : Mansell, 1993

_____

d. Halifax, N.S. : Nova Scotia Museum, 1997, c1976

_____

e. Berlin : Haude & Spener, 1989 printing, c1978

_____

f. Paris : Eiffel Publishing, c1985

_____

g. Barcelona : Moderna, 199-?

_____

h. San Francisco : Chronicle Books, 1994-1996

_____

i. New York : McGraw-Hill, 1997

_____

j. Moskva : Nauka, 1988?

_____

k. Auckland : Southern Publishing, 19--

_____

l. Amsterdam : Holland Books, between 1982 and 1984

_____

m. Melbourne : Wombat Press, ca. 1978

_____

n. Athens : Empire Press, 1983 [distributed] 1984

_____

o. Edinburgh : Highland Press, 197-

_____

EXERCISE 4.10

Complete the call number by assigning a main entry cutter and date for the following titles. The author and the date of publication are in parentheses.

a. International newcomer's guide to Boston
    (Rugendyke, 1997)

F
73
.18

b. Marketing design consultancy services (1998)	NK 1173
c. Ergonomics Conference (1992 : Berlin, Germany) Office ergonomics (1993)	TA 166
d. Ergonomics Conference (1997 : Cape Town, South Africa) Global ergonomics (1998)	TA 166
e. Medical screening handbook (Jacobs, 1995)	RA 427 .5
f. Elementary music theory (edited by Grutz, 1995)	MT 7
g. Texas Association of Museums. Future directions (1986)	AM 7
h. World Tourism Leaders' Meeting on the Social Impacts of Tourism (1997 : Manila, Philippines) Proceedings (1998)	G 154 .9

i. Handbook of photography (Kozloff, 1986)	TR 642
j. Handbook of photography (Kozloff, 1990)	TR 642
k. Dictionary of North American Indian tribes (1972)	E 76 .2
l. Genealogical Association of Nova Scotia. Directory of members (1990)	CS 88 .N8
m. International Association of Professional Photographers. Photography as a profession (1994)	TR 154
n. The American Civil War: a handbook of literature and research (edited by Woodworth, 1996)	E 456
o. International women in design (1993)	NK 1174

Shelflisting

Once a call number is constructed, the next step is to check the shelflist to see if the call number fits into your library's shelf arrangement. The shelflist is the record of the works in a library, in the order in which they are shelved.

In many cases the cutter number needs to be adjusted, whether you have constructed the number yourself or are using the LC number from a MARC record.

The following shelflist from an online catalog shows works on the topic of "design education" with cutter numbers based on titles, personal authors, and corporate authors:

1.	NK1170.B87 1990	The business of design
2.	NK1170.C68 1979	Council for National Academic Awards
3.	NK1170.C73 1990	Cranbrook design discourse
4.	NK1170.D47 1987	Design and aesthetics
5.	NK1170.D63 1978	Dodd, Mark
6.	NK1170.E34 1976	Eggleston, John
7.	NK1170.G74 1974	Great Britain. Dept. of Design Education
8.	NK1170.G75 1974	Green, Petra
9.	NK1170.M35 1977	Maier, Manfred. Basic principles of design
10.	NK1170.M35 1980	Maier, Manfred. Basic principles of design

Not all the cutter numbers conform exactly with the LC Cutter Table. The LC Cutter Table is used as a guide for creating a cutter number. You will often need to adjust the cutter number depending on how similar works have been cuttered in your shelflist in the past.

Adjusting the Cutter Number

Look at these examples from the list above:

7.	NK1170.G74 1974	Great Britain. Dept. of Design Education
8.	NK1170.G75 1974	Green, Petra

- "Great Britain" is cuttered according to the LC Cutter Table as .G74
- "Green, Petra" would also be cuttered according to the Table as .G74
- But we need to have a unique number and we also need to maintain the alphabetical shelf order, so
  .G74 for "Green" is adjusted to .G75.

The shelflist mirrors the arrangement of the works on the shelves as follows:

NK	NK	NK	NK	NK	NK	NK	NK	NK	NK
1170	1170	1170	1170	1170	1170	1170	1170	1170	1170
.B87	.C68	.C73	.D47	.D63	.E34	.G74	.G75	.M35	.M35
1990	1979	1990	1987	1978	1976	1974	1974	1977	1980

Exercise 4.11

Construct a call number based on the class number NK1170. Use the LC Cutter Table to assign a cutter number based on the main entry in the following works on "design education". Add the appropriate date to complete your call number.

a. Eaton, John. Design courses in the UK (1996)

| NK |
| 1170 |

b. Cargill, Anne. Tertiary programs for designers (1994)

| NK |
| 1170 |

c. Byers, Max. Educating designers (1995)

| NK |
| 1170 |

d. Council for Design Education (1985)

| NK |
| 1170 |

e. Design and art education in schools (1989)

| NK |
| 1170 |

f. Green, Roger. Design in higher education (1982)

| NK |
| 1170 |

g. Design italiano (1990)

NK 1170

h. Cunningham, Diane. Design education
    guidelines (1984)

NK 1170

i. Design Education Symposium (1987 :
    Canberra College of Advanced Education)
    (1989)

NK 1170

EXERCISE 4.12

Add the call numbers in Exercise 4.11 to the shelflist below. Adjust the cutter number when necessary.

a. NK1170.B87 1990   The business of design

b. _____

c. _____

d. _____

e. NK1170.C68 1979   Council for National Academic Awards

f. NK1170.C73 1990   Cranbrook design discourse

g. _____

h. NK1170.D47 1987   Design and aesthetics

i. _____

j. _____

k. _____

l. NK1170.D63 1978   Dodd, Mark

m. _____

n. NK1170.E34 1976   Eggleston, John

o. NK1170.G74 1974   Great Britain. Dept. of Design Education

p. NK1170.G75 1974   Green, Petra

q. _____

r. NK1170.M35 1977   Maier, Manfred. Basic principles of design

s. NK1170.M35 1980   Maier, Manfred. Basic principles of design

Authors with More than One Work at the Same Number

When an author has a number of books on one topic which are classified at the same number, works are subarranged alphabetically by title, by appending a digit to the author's cutter number.

For example, for works by Edward De Bono at the same class number:

BF441.D38 1977	Good thinking
BF441.D383 1990	The mechanism of mind
BF441.D385 1985	Six thinking hats
BF441.D386 1990	Thinking skills for success

When digits are appended to the author cutter number, space must be left for other titles to be added, especially when the author is a prolific writer on that topic.

An author will not necessarily have the same cutter number throughout the shelflist. The cutter number for the author depends on the alphabetical arrangement at a class number.

EXERCISE 4.13

Using the LC Cutter Table, provide a cutter number for the following works by Edward De Bono so that they fit alphabetically at the class number BF455. The first title in the shelflist is provided. The date of publication is in parentheses.

a. BF455.D363 1982   De Bono's thinking course

b. BF455_____   Learn to think (1982)

c.   BF455_____   New think: the use of lateral thinking (1968)

d.   BF455_____   PO: beyond yes and no (1973)

e.   BF455_____   Practical thinking (1991)

f.   BF455_____   Teaching thing (1976)

EXERCISE 4.14

The following authors have works classified at the same class number. Using the LC Cutter Table, assign cutter numbers for each of the authors in the list so that their works will shelve in correct alphabetical order.

a. MacDonald	.M33
b. MacDonnell	
c. MacIntosh	
d. MacMillan	
e. MacNaughton	
f. McCarthy	
g. McCartney	.M442
h. McFarland	
i. McKenzie	
j. McMahon	
k. McManus	.M47

EXERCISE 4.15

Build a complete call number. The author and the date of publication are in parentheses.

You will need to:
- identify the subject in the title
- select the appropriate schedule
- use the index or outline in the schedule to find the correct LC number
- assign the main entry cutter using the Cutter Table
- add the date in parentheses as the date of publication.

a. Current research in preschool education
    (Smith, 1997)

b. Private school education in Canada (Tippet, 1994)

c. Education of Amish children (Erickson, 1992)

d. Teacher placements in rural communities
    (van Oosten, 1993)

e. Giving birth to twins (Currier, 1998)

f. Diagnosing epilepsy (Andreevich, 1990)

g.   The elderly and surgery (Xiao, 1986)

h.   Incidence of tuberculosis in Afro-Americans (Underwood, 1989)

i.   History of printing in France (Perrault, 1985)

j.   Job descriptions for librarians (Fernandez, 1994)

k.   The importance of signs in libraries (Todd, 1989)

l.   Dictionary of words and phrases for the information superhighway (1999)

m.   The microbiology of toxoplasmosis (Hardy, 1994)

n.   An introduction to nuclear geology
(Rudnicki, 1991)

o.   The ecology of mangrove swamps (Cullen, 1995)

Special Types of Cutters

In addition to main entry cutters, there are several special types:

- title cutters
- corporate author cutters
- periodical "A" cutters
- topical cutters
- shelving cutters
- area cutters
- double cutters.

Title Cutters

As we have seen, title cutters are used when the title in the bibliographic record is the main entry. Another important use of title cutters is for literary works.

The call number below is for the novel *The prime of Miss Jean Brodie* by the English novelist Muriel Spark:

PR
6037
.P29
.P7
1961

PR	English literature
6037	Individual authors 1900-1960 - surname beginning with the letter "S"
.P29	Author cutter number based on the second letter of the author's surname: S**p**ark
.P7	Title cutter (usually only one digit is used) - use the LC Cutter Table
1961	Date of publication

Other works by Muriel Spark will be classified at the same number—PR6037.P29—followed by a title cutter for each work. All works by the same author are shelved alphabetically by title.

Other Points Worth Noting

- Not all author numbers are listed in the P schedule.
  - It is useful to check the Library of Congress catalog for an author number.
  - If you have to assign a new cutter number for an author, use as a guide the cutter numbers already established for authors in the schedule and your shelflist.
- Some authors write under more than one name. If Spark used another name for some of her works, they would still be classified together with her other works at the above number.
- Some authors write in more than one language, or may write while resident in another country. Classify works in a particular language with the literature of that language. If the author was resident in a particular country while writing a work, classify that work with the literature of that country.

EXERCISE 4.16

Provide title cutters for the following works by Muriel Spark and create a call number. The date in parentheses is the date of publication. The first part of the call number is PR6037.P29.

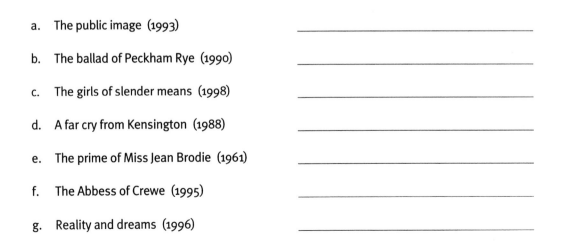

a. The public image (1993) _____

b. The ballad of Peckham Rye (1990) _____

c. The girls of slender means (1998) _____

d. A far cry from Kensington (1988) _____

e. The prime of Miss Jean Brodie (1961) _____

f. The Abbess of Crewe (1995) _____

g. Reality and dreams (1996) _____

h. The comforters (1994)   _____

i. The prime of Miss Jean Brodie (1994)   _____

Exercise 4.17

List the works in Exercise 4.16 in correct shelf order.

a.	b.	c.	d.	e.
f.	g.	h.	i.	

Corporate Author Cutters

The Library of Congress has developed its own policy for cuttering corporate bodies. Consult the *Subject Cataloging Manual. Shelflisting* for more details. Your library may have a different cuttering policy for corporate bodies.

These are some of the features of the Library of Congress policy:
*   Assign the same cutter number to publications cataloged under a corporate body heading. Cutter for the first word of the main entry. Disregard the title. This means that these works will be arranged by the date of publication.

For example, the Center for Freshwater Ecology (U.S.) has published three works on the topic of freshwater ecology. The cutter number for the Center is .C46:

Principles and applications of freshwater ecology	QH541.5.F7.C46 1993
Freshwater ecosystems	QH541.5.F7.C46 1996
The decline of freshwater ecosystems	QH541.5.F7.C46 1999

*   Ignore all subheadings for a corporate body when cuttering. Cutter for the corporate body.

For example, the British Tourist Authority has two subheadings. In the following three examples, the cutter number is the same because the subheading is ignored. The cutter number for the authority is .B75. This means that all works for the different units of the authority are intershelved at one number:

British Tourist Authority *Annual report* (1995)	G155.G7.B75 1995
British Tourist Authority. Accommodation Unit. *Statistical survey* (1997)	G155.G7.B75 1997
British Tourist Authority. Travel Unit. *Survey of incoming tourists* (1998)	G155.G7.B75 1998

- If more than one publication on the same topic is issued by the same corporate body in a given year, add a work letter to the date starting with "a" and continuing through the alphabet in order of receipt.

For example, the Australian Heritage Commission published three works on the same topic in the same year. The work letter indicates the date of receipt:

The heritage of Australia (1997)	DU94.A88 1997
The national estate (1997)	DU94.A88 1997a
The national register of heritage buildings (1997)	DU94.A88 1997b

- When the main entry begins with the name of a country or other jurisdictional name followed by a division or agency of that government, the cutter number is based on the jurisdiction and the first subheading only.

In the following example, the cutter number is the same for the three branches of the Ministry of Finance. However, the Task Force has a different cutter number:

Ontario. Ministry of Finance. Administration Branch. *Property tax relief in Ontario* (1991)	HJ4293.O64 1991
Ontario. Ministry of Finance. Financial Planning Branch. *Report on equalized assessment* (1993)	HJ4293.O64 1993
Ontario. Ministry of Finance. Statistics Branch. *Statistical survey of real property tax* (1997)	HJ4293.O64 1997
Ontario. Task Force on Equalization and Assessment. *Final report* (1995)	HJ4293.O68 1995

Periodical "A" cutters

An "A" cutter is used in the schedules for periodicals. This is like a shelving cutter, so that all periodicals on a topic are brought together on the shelves at the beginning of that topic. Sometimes periodicals are given a specific class number and an "A" cutter is not used (see Example 2).

Example 1

RA	Public aspects of medicine
	Personal health and hygiene
	Personal health and grooming guides for classes of people
	Women
778.A1	Periodicals. Societies. Serials
778.A2-Z	General works

A periodical with the title *Healthright* is classified as follows:

RA	
778	
.A1	cutter for periodicals
.H43	cutter for main entry title, *Healthright*

The second cutter is for the main entry (usually the title of the journal). The date of publication is not added.

Example 2

A class number is used specifically for periodicals:

QA	Mathematics
	Electronic computers. Computer science
	Computer software
76.75	Periodicals. Societies. Serials

A periodical called *Software process improvement and practice* will be classified as follows:

QA	
76	number assigned for periodicals on this topic
.75	
.S64	main entry cutter for title, *Software process improvement and practice*

Sometimes periodicals are classified at a "general works" number. This occurs when only a few numbers exist at a topic.

EXERCISE 4.18

Find the class number for periodicals on the following topics.

a.   Mathematical logic _____

b.   Micrometeorology _____

c.   Textile bleaching _____

d.   The study and teaching of home economics _____

e.   Experimental psychology _____

f.   Psychoanalysis _____

g.   Christian ethics _____

h.   Philosophy of genealogy _____

Topical Cutters

Topical cutters arrange individual topics in alphabetical order when a series of topics does not lend itself to a logical or hierarchical order. They are also used when there is a shortage of integer or decimal numbers. Captions for topics reflect LCSH terminology where possible.

Often the topical cutter is given in the schedules. Occasionally, you will need to create one.

Instructions for topical cutters typically appear as:
- Special topics, A-Z
- Special subjects, A-Z
- Special, A-Z
- Other, A-Z.

They can be more specific:
- Special objects, A-Z
- Special aspects or movements, A-Z
- By breed, A-Z
- By type of environment, A-Z.

NC	DRAWING. DESIGN. ILLUSTRATION	NC
1849.A-Z	Special topics, A-Z Class here general works on the topics as well as works on the topics in a particular region, country, etc.	
1849.A29	Advertising	
1849.A35	Airlines	
1849.A44	Alcoholic beverages	
1849.A46	Alps	
1849.A53	Animals	
1849.A76	Art exhibitions	
1849.A95	Automobiles	
1849.B35	Banks and banking	
1849.B43	Beer	
1849.B52	Bicycles	
1849.B57	Birth control	
1849.B84	Bullfights	
	Cigarettes, see NC1849.T63	
	Cigars, see NC1849.T63	
1849.C57	Circus	
1849.C63	Coca-Cola Company	
1849.D35	Dance	
1849.E84	Etiquette	
1849.F38	Fashion	

A work by Walters (1998) on dance posters would be classified at:

NC	Drawing. Design. Illustration
1849	special topics on posters
.D35	topical cutter for dance posters listed in schedule
.W35	main entry cutter for author, Walters
1998	date of publication

LCC lists many topics, and new editions of schedules appear to be increasingly enumerative for special topics. However, sometimes you will have to create topical cutters. When you create them, make sure they fit into the list of topics that already exist and record your decision in the schedules.

Shelving Cutters

These cutters are provided in the schedules or in the tables of a schedule. They are used to shelve some categories of works before others at a given class number.

Example 1

```
HT       Communities. Classes. Races
              Abolition of slavery
1029          Biography of abolitionists
.A3               Collective
.A4-Z             Individual, A-Z
```

This means that:
- all collective biographies of abolitionists are shelved at .A3 plus a main entry cutter
- individual biographies are cuttered by the subject (person) plus a main entry cutter.

Note that a biography about Abrams could not be cuttered at .A2 but would need a cutter number starting at least at .A4.

A biography of Victor Schoelcher (Braun, 1983) would be classified as follows:

```
HT
1029
.S36     cutter for Schoelcher
.B73     main entry cutter for author, Braun
1983     date of publication
```

Example 2

Different types of works are grouped together by means of a shelving cutter:

```
NC       Drawing. Design. Illustration
997           Commercial art. Advertising art
.A1               Periodicals
.A2               Congresses
.A3A-Z            Collections. By collector or institution, A-Z
.A4A-Z            Exhibitions. By place, A-Z
.A5               General works
```

The following table illustrates the use of shelving cutters taken from Example 2 above:

Example	Instruction	Call Number
Graphic design magazine	.A1 Periodicals + main entry cutter	NC 997 .A1 .G73
Symposium on the history of graphic design held in 1983	.A2 Congresses + main entry cutter + date of congress	NC 997 .A2 .S935 1983
Wm. Frost Mobley's visual history of the advertising trade: a collection (1981)	.A3 Collections + cutter by "Collector or institution, A-Z" + expansion based on the main entry + date of publication	NC 997 .A3 .M636 1981
Designer's self image. An exhibition held in Jerusalem (Marcus, 1991)	.A4 Exhibitions + cutter for place of exhibition + expansion based on the main entry + date of publication	NC 997 .A4 .J46 1991
Urban entertainment graphics (Hunt, 1997)	.A5 General works + main entry cutter + date of publication	NC 997 .A5 .H86 1997

EXERCISE 4.19

Use the following excerpts to answer the questions.

RA565	Environmental health		BF109	Psychology	
.A1	Periodicals			Biography	
.A2	Congresses		.A1	Collective	
.A3-Z	General works		.A2-Z	Individual, A-Z	

a.   What is the shelving cutter for a journal on environmental health?

b. What is the class number and shelving cutter for conferences on environmental health?

c. Provide a call number for a textbook on environmental health by an author with the surname Aaronsen, published in 1994.

d. Which is the correct call number for the title *Environmental health handbook* (Abard, 1992)?

	1.		2.		3.
	RA		RA		RA
	565		565		565
	.A3		.A33		.A23
	.A23		1992		1992
	1992				

e. Identify the class number and shelving cutter for a work about the lives of six notable German psychologists.

Area Cutters

Instructions for cuttering by a country, area or place typically appear as:

- By region or country, A-Z
- By region or state, A-Z
- By city, A-Z
- By region, country, county, etc., A-Z
- By region or province, A-Z
- Other countries, A-Z
- Special countries, A-Z.

Note that the instruction "By country, A-Z" is being phased out of use. Where it appears, interpret it as "By region or country, A-Z".

The following excerpt from SB470.5 Landscape gardening. Landscape architecture illustrates the use of these instructions:

SB	Plant culture
	Landscape gardening. Landscape architecture
	History and conditions
470.5	General works
	By region or country
	United States
470.53	General works
470.54.A-Z	By region or state, A-Z
470.55.A-Z	Other regions or countries, A-Z

Example 1

A work on the history of landscape architecture in Alabama (Dittmer, 1996) is cuttered at .A2, as the instruction provides for cuttering by state in the United States:

SB	
470	
.54	decimal extension for "By region or state, A-Z"
.A2	cutter for Alabama
.D58	main entry cutter for author
1996	date of publication

If there is no established cutter number in your shelflist for an American state or Canadian province, refer to the tables for American states and Canadian provinces in the Library of Congress *Subject Cataloging Manual. Shelflisting* to establish your cutter number.

However, you may need to adjust it depending on other numbers in the same alphabetical sequence.

There is also a table for regions and countries in the shelflisting manual.

Example 2

A work on the history of landscape architecture in Australia (Herrick, 1994):

SB	
470	
.55	decimal extension for "Other regions or countries, A-Z"
.A8	cutter for Australia
.H47	main entry cutter
1994	date of publication

EXERCISE 4.20

Use the excerpt from SB470.5 Landscape gardening and the LC Cutter Table, and construct a complete call number for the following titles. The author and the date of publication are in parentheses.

a.   Landscape architecture in Ohio (Green, 1992)

b.   Landscape beautification in Italy's cities (Fontana, 1986)

c.   European gardens in the twentieth century (Stepnik, 1990)

d.   Pennsylvania's landscape architecture (Fuller, 1988)

e.   History of landscape architecture in Denmark (Lund, 1995)

f.   Landscape tradition of Sri Lanka (1991)

g.   History of landscape beautification in Sydney, New South Wales (Taylor, 1987)

h. History of landscape gardening in the
    Cayman Islands (Dal Santo, 1994)

Double Cutters

Double cuttering is the use of two cutter numbers in building a call number.

Example 1

We have a book titled *Career development* by Jones, published in 1997.

There is a cutter for the topic and a cutter for the main entry:

HF	Commerce
5549	Personnel management. Employment management
.5	decimal extension "By topic, A-Z"
.C35	cutter #1: topical cutter for Career development
.J66	cutter #2: cutter for main entry author, Jones
1997	date of publication

Example 2

This book is *The design of Austrian insignia* (Bellini, 1989).

There is a cutter for the country and a cutter for the main entry:

NK	Decorative Arts. Applied Arts. Decoration and Ornament
7415	History of crown jewels, insignia, regalia: "Other countries, A-Z"
.A8	cutter #1: by country, Austria
.B45	cutter #2: cutter for main entry author, Bellini
1989	date of publication

The schedules contain different combinations of two cutters. These are some of them:
*   area cutter   +   institution
*   topic   +   institution
*   topic   +   artist.

When you have two such cutters, you cannot add another line for a title or main entry cutter. The second cutter must be expanded to the right to accommodate the main entry cutter and to avoid a triple cutter.

No more than two cutters can be used. Triple cuttering is NOT allowed.

Example 3
Let's say we have a work titled *Prison labor in Lagos, Nigeria* (Smith, 1990):

HV	Social Pathology. Social and Public Welfare. Criminology
8931	Prison labor: "Other regions or countries, A-Z"
.N62	cutter #1: area cutter for Nigeria
.L3	cutter #2: local area cutter for Lagos
1990	date of publication

This call number already has two cutters. We cannot add another line for the main entry cutter, Smith. We must expand the .L3 (Lagos) cutter.

Procedure
1. Take the first letter of the main entry cutter, Smith
2. Go to paragraph (5) of the LC Cutter Table to find the value of the first letter
   S = 7
3. Append this digit to the second cutter
   .L37

Title	CORRECT	INCORRECT
Prison labor in Lagos, Nigeria	HV 8931 .N62 .L37 1990	HV 8931 .N62 .L3 .S65 1990

Double cuttering with a second cutter expansion arises most often when you use tables. Further examples and exercises will follow in Chapter 5.

Chapter 5
TABLES

Introduction
Tables are used in LCC for two main reasons:
- to save space by not repeating the same instruction throughout the schedule
- to allow you to assign a more specific number.

Tables are included in almost all the schedules. Some schedules—in particular H, N, P, B and L—use them more often and contain more tables in the back of the individual volumes. The P schedule also has a separate publication called *Language and Literature Tables*.

There are tables which apply generally across all schedules, and also tables which apply only to specific subjects or subclasses. Some schedules rely heavily on tables within the main body of the classification, and other schedules contain a significant number of tables at the end of the main body (before the index).

This chapter starts with the simplest tables and progresses to the more complex. It covers:
- type 1 table - table within the schedules
- type 2 table - table within the schedules
- type 3 table - table within the schedules
- type 4 table - table within the schedules + table at back of schedule
- Biography Table - special table used generally across all schedules
- Translation Table - special table used generally across all schedules
- *Language and Literature Tables* - separate publication for the P schedules.

EXERCISE 5.1
You need to look at several schedules to answer these questions.

a. How many tables are in the back of the Q schedule?

b. Does the table of QC60.A2-Z allow you to specify a city?

c. Can you cutter for the United States at QC47.A-Z?

d.   At the same QC area, where would you put works for regions or states in the United States?

e.   Still at the QC area, where would you put Developing countries?

f.   How many tables are in the back of the H schedule?

g.   What is Table H15?

h.   Look at Tables H15, H16 and H17. What is the difference?
     (Hint: Look at the headings.)

i.   At HS1721-1725, which table should you apply for Spanish-American societies?

j.   At HJ77, under Japan, does the table you are referred to provide instructions for general serials?

k.   At HV6604.A-Z, is there an instruction in the table for arrangement by kidnapper's name?

l.   At TF6.A2-Z, what table does the schedule refer you to?

m.   At TC558.A-Z, is there an instruction for special dams in other regions or countries?

n.   At S599.8.A-Z, are there instructions for island groups?

o.   At S599.8.A-Z, what is the instruction for *Local, A-Z*?

p.   How many tables are there in the back of the N schedule?

q.   What does Table N10 allow you to do?

r.   What is Table N5?

s.   At NK8213-8296.3 Other countries, what two tables are you referred to?

t.   At LB1244-1246, how many numbers are available for Mexico?

u.   At the same LB area, what arrangement is available for the third number?

v.   At LC624.A3-Z, what is the instruction for *Local, A-Z*?

w.   At LC561-586.2, what number would you use for a Lutheran periodical?

x.   Still at the LC area, what number would you use for a general work for the Friends denomination?

y.   At BL1313.2-29, the instruction for Table 1 has a footnote. Follow the instruction in the footnote. How many tables are you referred to?

z.   Look at the tables in the back of the BL, BM, BP, BQ schedule. Note the different formats of the tables.

Types of Tables

Type 1

In this type of table, we will use:
- a table within the schedule
- the LC Cutter Table.

Example 1

> HE   Transportation and Communications
> >   Urban transportation
> >   By region or country
> 311   Other regions or countries, A-Z
> >   *Under each country:*
> >   *.x   General works*
> >   *.x2A-Z   Local, A-Z*

Let's say we have a book about Canada's urban transportation development strategy.

The instruction "Other regions or countries, A-Z" tells us that other countries should be cuttered alphabetically. Use the LC Cutter Table in Chapter 4 to work out the cutter.

> the cutter for Canada is .C2
> the *.x* is now replaced by .C2

Note: When creating a country cutter using tables, it is normal to use only one digit:

Canada	.C2	*not*	.C26
United States	.U6	*not*	.U65

The call number for a general work on urban transportation in Canada would be:

> HE
> 311
> .C2
> main entry cutter
> date of publication

This means that books on urban transportation in Canada will begin with HE311.C2.

EXERCISE 5.2

Go to the number in the relevant schedule and construct the call number following the instructions in the table. Use the instruction for general works. The author and the date of publication are in parentheses.

a. TJ603.4.A-Z
     The history of locomotives in Mexico
     (Thompson, 1972)

b. SF243.5.A-Z
     Research into the teaching of dairying in
     Vermont (Cruzic, 1983)

c. HM22.A-Z
     History of sociology in France
     (Grenier, 1991)

d. N5208.A-Z
     Art patronage in Italy (Sergi, 1994)

e. NA6862.A-Z
     Design of amphitheaters in Thailand
     (Halangahu, 1989)

f. QD47.5.A-Z
     Chemistry laboratory manuals used in
     Iowa (Schultz, 1996)

g. RA413.5.A-Z
     Private medical care plans in Great Britain
     (MacDonald, 1995)

h. LB3491.A-W
   Open air schools in Arizona
   (Utzon, 1981)

Example 2

Now let's say that we have a book about urban transportation in Ottawa (written by Hutcheon, published in 1988). Refer again to the table at HE311 above. We need to follow the instructions for *Local, A-Z*:

Instructions	Example	Building the Call Number
Other regions or countries, A-Z *Under each country*: **.x2**A-Z *Local, A-Z*	**.x** = .C2 (the cutter for Canada) **.x2** = **.C22** (cutter for local areas in Canada)	HE 311 **.C22**
.x2**A-Z** *Local, A-Z* Cutter the local area alphabetically - put this cutter on a new line preceded by a decimal point	.O88 is the cutter for Ottawa	HE 311 .C22 **.O88**
Main entry cutter - you must expand to the right because you cannot have more than two cutters	1. Take the first letter of the main entry cutter, **H**utcheon 2. Go to paragraph (5) of the Cutter Table to find the value of the first letter H = 4 3. Append 4 after the second cutter (local area cutter)	HE 311 .C22 .O88**4**
	Add the date of publication	HE 311 .C22 .O884 **1988**

If you browse the shelves at HE311.C2, you will first find all the general works about urban transportation in Canada. Then you will find all the works about urban transportation in Canada in local areas at HE311.C22. The local areas will be arranged alphabetically.

Note

Schedules are not consistent, and instructions are written in different ways. Note these equivalents:

.x	=	.xA - .xZ
.x2A-Z	=	.x2A - .x2Z
.x3A-Z	=	.x3A - .x3Z
.x4A-Z	=	.x4A - .x4Z

EXERCISE 5.3

Go to the number in the relevant schedule and construct the call number following the instructions in the table at that number. The author and the date of publication are in parentheses.

a. HG1939.A-Z
    Saving banks in Madrid, Spain
    (Florez, 1997)

b. LC929.3.A-Z
    Buddhist education in Bangkok, Thailand
    (Laothamatas, 1982)

c. QD2.A2-Z
    Chemical museums in San Francisco
    (Jackson, 1989)

d. NA7858.A-Z
    The design of Maxim's Restaurant in Paris,
    France (King, 1985)

e. NC998.6.A-Z
    Graphic design in Beijing in the twentieth
    century (Scott, 1990)

f. QK480.A-Z
    The botany of the Waite Arboretum in
    Adelaide, Australia (Wrigley, 1988)

g. HF5469.23.A-Z
    Current business issues facing
    supermarkets in Atlanta, Georgia
    (Alderman, 1998)

h. RA523.A-Z
    Public health problems in Athens, Greece
    (Adamopoulos, 1994)

i. RA630.A-Z
    The by-laws regulating cemeteries in
    Jakarta, Indonesia (Anwar, 1991)

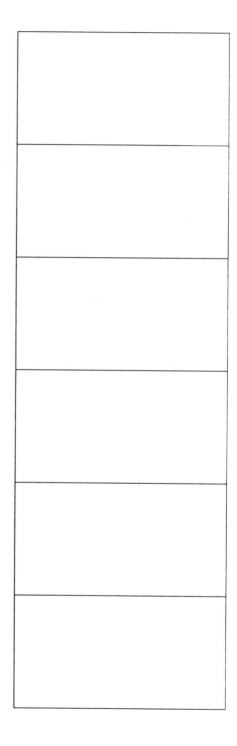

Example 3

The following excerpt gives an additional instruction for cuttering under country by type of waterway:

HE	Transportation and Communications
	Water transportation
389.A-Z	By region or country, A-Z
	Under each country:
.x	*General works*
.x2	*Inland*
.x3	*Ports*
.x4A-Z	*Special waterways, rivers whose course is entirely within the limits of one country, A-Z*

The following table illustrates the use of the cutters taken from Example 3 above:

Instructions in Schedule	Example	Call Number
By region or country, A-Z *Under each country:* .x *General works*	A general work on British waterways (Mason, 1969) The country cutter for Great Britain is .G7, so .x = <u>.G7</u>	HE 389 <u>.G7</u> .M37 1969
By region or country, A-Z *Under each country:* .x2 *Inland*	A work on British inland waterways (Jobson, 1975) Append 2 to the country cutter, so .x2 = <u>.G72</u>	HE 389 <u>.G72</u> .J63 1975
By region or country, A-Z *Under each country:* .x3 *Ports*	A work on British ports (Dickson, 1986) Append 3 to the country cutter, so .x3 = <u>.G73</u>	HE 389 <u>.G73</u> .D53 1986

| By region or country, A-Z Under each country
.x4A-Z   *Special waterways, etc.* | A work on the River Tyne (Adams, 1990)

Append 4 to the country cutter, so
.x4   =   <u>.G74</u>

The second cutter - <u>.T96</u> - is for the local area (River Tyne)

Remember to expand the second cutter for the main entry | HE
389
<u>.G74</u>
<u>.T963</u>
1990 |

EXERCISE 5.4

Go to the number in the relevant schedule and construct the call number following the instructions in the table at that number. The author and the date of publication are in parentheses.

a.   LB475.A-Z
     Biography and criticism of Ezekiel
     Cheever (Polak, 1990)

b.   HJ5715.A-Z
     Sales tax in Quebec (Preville, 1994)

c.   SF83.A-Z
     Research in animal culture at the Royal
     Veterinary College, London
     (Sinclair, 1986)

d.   HF5465.A-Z
     Department stores in New York
     (Carpenter, 1992)

e. QC47.A-Z
The teaching of physics at the University
of Toronto (Faggioni, 1995)

f. BJ2007.A-Z
Japanese etiquette for students
(Takachi, 1984)

Type 2

In this type of table, we will use:
- a table within the schedule
- the LC Cutter Table.

HB	Economic theory. Demography
	History of economics
	History of economic theory
101-130	By region or country
	Under each country:
.A2	*History*
.A3	*Collective biography*
.A5-.Z	*Individual biography, A-Z*

In this type of table, cutters cannot start before a given letter and number because previous letters and numbers have specific meanings and functions.

For example, the instruction for individual biography is .A5-.Z. This means that you cannot start a cutter number before .A5.

If the person's name is Abraham, you would cutter him or her as .A27 according to the LC Cutter Table. But your first cutter can only start at .A5.

Your library may acquire a book by Aarons. If you already have a book by Abraham (at the same class number) at .A5, then you will have problems fitting in Aarons.

Sometimes you may have to reclassify items so that new ones can fit in. If you reclassified the work by Abraham to .A53, then you could cutter Aarons at .A52. That would still leave space for other authors also starting with the letters "Aa" and "Abr".

Sometimes a third digit is needed to fit a work into the shelflist.

Note

Schedules are not consistent, and instructions are written in different ways. Note these equivalents:

.xA4-.xZ	=	.xA4-Z
.xA6-.xZ	=	.xA6-Z

Exercise 5.5

Go to the number in the relevant schedule and construct the call number following the instructions in the table at that number. The author and the date of publication are in parentheses.

a. LB2803.2.A-Z
    List of school officials in Abakira, Japan
    (Shinoda, 1991)

b. N7433.4.A-Z
    Julie Bradley: a biography (Clarke, 1989)

c. HB101-130
    John Hewson: biography of an Australian
    economist (Willis, 1986)

d. HV5831.A-Z
    Drug habits in Minnesota (Abbey, 1999)

Type 3

In this type of table, we will use:

- a table within the schedule
- the LC Cutter Table.

You are often referred to this type of table by an "Apply table at" note.

R	Medicine (General)	
	History	
	By region or country	
461-684	Other regions or countries	
	Under each region or country:	
	1	*General works*
	2	*General special*
	3	*Local, A-Z*
	4.A-4.Z	*Biography*
	4.A1A-4.A1Z	*Collective*
	4.A2-4.Z	*Individual, A-Z*

Let's say that we have several works about the history of medicine in various countries. These works are classified between R461-684. Regions and countries have been assigned a range of numbers in this part of the schedule.

South America is assigned four numbers: R480-483. This is how South America appears in the schedules at R461-684:

480-483	South America
	Apply table at R461-684

This is how you assign numbers in this range:

Instruction from Schedule	What it means	Example
1 General works	Assign the first number of the range (R480) to *General works*	History of medicine in South America (Morello, 1982) R **480** .M67 1982
2 General special	Assign the second number of the range (R481) to *General special*	History of 18th century medicine in South America (Dalbo, 1975) R **481** .D35 1975
3 Local, A-Z	Assign the third number of the range (R482) for a locality, and add a cutter for that locality (A-Z)	History of medicine in Bolivia (Llardo, 1961) R **482** **.B6** .L43 1961
4.A-4.Z Biography *4.A1A-4.A1Z Collective*	Assign the fourth number of the range (R483) when you have a biography - Take the fourth number (R483) - Add the shelving cutter .A1 - Add the cutter for the main entry (A-Z) Note that you cannot include notation for both Bolivia and a collective biography	A group biography of doctors in Bolivia (Sousa, 1988) R **483** **.A1** **.S68** 1988

Biography 4.A2-4.Z *Individual, A-Z*	- Take the fourth number (R483) - Add the cutter for the subject of the biography (note that you cannot use .A1—start at .A2) - Add the main entry cutter	A biography of Perez (Sousa, 1992) R <u>483</u> <u>.P47</u> <u>.S68</u> 1990

Exercise 5.6

This exercise is based on R461-684. Build call numbers for the following works. The author and the date of publication are in parentheses.

a. A history of medicine in the West Indies (1985)

b. A history of Icelandic medical practitioners (Rey, 1994)

c. Moscow doctors in the post-war period (Popov, 1972)

d. A history of medical services and hospitals in Ireland (Mulligan, 1984)

e. Biography and personal philosophy of a retired Indian physician, Dr. Desh Singh (Hunter, 1995)

f. Saudi medical bibliography, 1970-1980
    (Madkour, 1983)

g. A lifetime in China: Arthur Chung's story
    (Tein, 1969)

h. A history of Sri Lankan physicians
    (Wickramasinghe, 1973)

i. Warsaw doctors: a history of their move
    towards reform (Krywoszyja, 1990)

j. A history of doctors in Chad (Duroux, 1981)

EXERCISE 5.7

Apply the instructions to the numbers indicated and build call numbers for the following works. The author and the date of publication are in parentheses.

a. R155-363
    A social history of medicine in Hawaii (Le, 1986)

b.   R155-363
     A history of general practice in Houston,
     Texas (Johnson, 1984)

c.   LC1751-2572
     The life of women students in Ecuador
     (Gonzalez, 1992)

d.   LC1751-2572
     Educational opportunities for women in
     Bucharest, Romania: a historical study
     (Czoban, 1995)

e.   LC561-586.2
     Religious education for Methodists
     (Childs, 1997)

f.   HS1701-1705
     Japanese clubs in San Francisco (Sato,
     1996)

g.   HS1701-1705
     Jewish societies in Australia (Perlman,
     1989)

h.   HV7250-7300
     Documentation for criminal justice in
     Bangor, Maine (Brown, 1993)

    i.   HV7250-7300
          Criminal justice documents in Aberdeen,
          Maryland (Regan, 1988)

Type 4

In this type of table, we will use:
- a table within the schedule
- a table at the back of the schedule to give us a country number
- the LC Cutter Table.

Example 1: *10 nos.*

Study this excerpt. Note that the instructions in this example do not apply to the United States, because specific numbers have been assigned to the United States.

	United States
3881	Periodicals. Societies. Serials
3885	General works
3887	Organization and administration
3887.5	Finance
3888	Public policy
3890.A-Z	By region or state, A-Z
4001-4420.7	Other regions or countries (Table H9)
	Add country number in table to HD4000
	Under each country:
	10 nos.
	1 Periodicals. Societies. Serials
	5 General works
	7 Organization and administration
	7.5 Finance
	8 Public policy
	10.A-Z Local, A-Z
	5 nos.
	1 Periodicals. Societies. Serials
	3 General works
	4 Public policy
	5.A-Z Local, A-Z
	1 no.
	.A1-.A5 Periodicals. Societies. Serials
	.A6-.Z7 General works
	.Z8A-Z Local, A-Z

Look at the numbers under the "Other regions or countries" caption. Note that in the *10 nos.* and *5 nos.* sections, not all numbers are used within those ranges. This allows for further expansion.

Let's say that we have a book about public corporations and public policy in Germany (1981):

Instructions from Schedule	Example	Building the Call Number
Table H9	171-180 Germany There are ten numbers assigned to Germany	
Add country number in table to HD4000 (this is the base number) "Add" means the mathematical operation	HD4000 + 171-180 = HD4171-4180	HD <u>4171-4180</u>
Look at the captions under *10 nos.* Select the category that matches the work 8 *Public policy*	Take the eighth number of the range for Germany: HD4178	HD <u>4178</u>
Add main entry cutter and date of publication	Title main entry, so cutter is .P83 Date of publication is 1981	HD 4178 <u>.P83</u> <u>1981</u>

EXERCISE 5.8

Find the country number or range of numbers for the following countries. Add this number or range of numbers to the base number HD4000 (according to the table at HD4001-4420.7).

a. Singapore _____

b. China _____

c. Bangladesh _____

d. Kenya _____

e.   Vietnam   _____

f.   Kuwait   _____

g.   Hungary   _____

h.   Cuba   _____

i.   Chile   _____

j.   Venezuela   _____

k.   Sweden   _____

l.   Greece   _____

m.   New Zealand   _____

n.   Bermuda   _____

EXERCISE 5.9

Calculate the class number for the following works. Use the 10 nos. section in HD4001-4420.7.

a.   General work about state industries in Canada   _____

b.   General work about public works in France   _____

c.   Finance in Germany   _____

d.   Organization and administration of state industries in
     Great Britain   _____

e.   Public policy in France   _____

f.   A serial about government ownership in Germany   _____

g.   Public works in Bristol, England   _____

h.   Public works in Montpellier, France   _____

i.   Government works in Dresden, Germany   _____

j.   Maintenance of government buildings in Saskatoon, Canada   _____

EXERCISE 5.10

Work out the complete call number for the following works. Use the 10 nos. section of HD4001-4420.7. The author and the date of publication are in parentheses.

a.   Administration and accountability for public services in Britain (Day, 1987)

b.   Developments in public policy in France (Beliveau, 1991)

c.   Power at the top: a critical survey of nationalized industries in Canada (Jenkins, 1983)
(Hint: Use the General works number.)

d.   New financial systems for public industries in Germany (Messerschmidt, 1986)

e.   Public enterprise in an era of change in Quebec, Canada (Richard, 1993)

f. Crown corporations as a problem in organization design in Scotland (Ferrand, 1996)

Example 2: *5 nos.*

Refer again to the excerpt from the HD schedule above. This time we will use the *5 nos.* part.

We have a work about the management of capital works projects in New Delhi, India (Rao, 1998):

Instructions from Schedule	Example	Building the Call Number
Table H9	291-295 India There are five numbers assigned to India	
Add country number in table to HD4000	HD4000 + 291-295 = HD4291-4295	HD <u>4291-4295</u>
Look at the captions under *5 nos.* Select the category that matches the work 5.A-Z *Local, A-Z*	Take the fifth number of the range for India: HD4295	HD <u>4295</u>
Cutter the local area (*Local, A-Z*)	New Delhi is .N4	HD 4295 <u>.N4</u>
Add main entry cutter and date of publication	Author main entry cutter is .R36 Date of publication is 1998	HD 4295 .N4 <u>.R36</u> <u>1998</u>

EXERCISE 5.11

Build a complete call number for the following works. Use the 5 nos. section of HD4001-4420.7 and use the number for General works. The author and the date of publication are in parentheses.

a.   China's management of state enterprises (Montgomery, 1985)

b.   Government business in India (Chatterjee, 1969)

c.   Private business and economic reform in Australia (Youens, 1995)

d.   Peruvian reforms in economic management (Jackson, 1992)

e.   Improving Indonesia's public enterprise performance (Keating, 1998)

EXERCISE 5.12

Build a complete call number. Use the 5 nos. section of HD4001-4420.7 and use the local instructions. The author and the date of publication are in parentheses.

a.   New public enterprises in Caracas, Venezuela (Silva, 1987)

b. Public industry efficiencies in Sydney, Australia (Morozow, 1993)

c. The role of financial manager in state enterprises in Zurich, Switzerland (Rogivue, 1991)

d. The performance evaluation of public enterprises in Lisbon, Portugal (Viegas, 1996)

e. A system for evaluating government companies in Manila, Philippines (Zosa, 1989)

Example 3: *1 no.*

Refer again to the excerpt from the HD schedule above. This time we have a one-number country.

Now we have a work about public works in Port Louis in Mauritius (Rose, 1989):

Instructions from Schedule	Example	Building the Call Number
Table H9	370.5 Mauritius There is one number assigned to Mauritius	

Instructions from Schedule	Example	Building the Call Number
Add country number in table to HD4000	HD4000 + 370.5 = HD4370.5	HD <u>4370</u> <u>.5</u>
Look at the captions under *1 no.* Select the category that matches the work .Z8A-Z *Local, A-Z*	Add .Z8 to the call number	HD 4370 .5 <u>.Z8</u>
Cutter the local area (*Local, A-Z*)	Port Louis is .P6	HD 4370 .5 .Z8 <u>.P6</u>
Add the main entry cutter and date of publication	There are already two cutters, so you will have to expand the second cutter to the right for the main entry cutter	HD 4370 .5 .Z8 .P6<u>Z</u> <u>1989</u>

Works about state industries or public works in Mauritius would be arranged on the shelves as follows:

Periodicals, Societies, Serials		General Works		Local Areas Arranged Alphabetically	
HD 4370 .5 .A1	HD 4370 .5 .A5	HD 4370 .5 .A6	HD 4370 .5 .Z7	HD 4370 .5 .Z8 .A...	HD 4370 .5 .Z8 .Z...

EXERCISE 5.13

Build a complete call number for the following works. Use the 1 no. section of HD4001-4420.7. The author and the date of publication are in parentheses.

a. An investigation into local authority trading activities in Poland (Lapinski, 1992)

b. Commercialization in the public sector in Monaco (Muspratt, 1989)

c. A history of public works in Greece (Spiros, 1995)

d. The challenge of corporatization of local government in the Bahamas (Lloyd, 1981)

e. State owned enterprises in Kathmandu, Nepal (Kenchington, 1998)

f. The scope for privatization in Hanoi, Vietnam (Nguyen, 1996)

g. The financing of local authority works in Kumasi, Ghana (Acheampong, 1990)

h.   Pricing policy in government factories in
      Auckland, New Zealand (Lange, 1987)

EXERCISE 5.14

Build a complete call number. Go to the range of numbers indicated and follow the instructions for tables.
The author and the date of publication are in parentheses.

a.   SF621-723
      History of veterinary medicine in North
      Carolina (Taylor, 1993)

b.   SF621-723
      History of veterinary medicine in
      Barcelona, Spain (Santana, 1986)

c.   LA1460-1464
      History of primary and secondary
      education in Lebanon (Barakat, 1981)

d.   NA7201-7477
      Domestic architecture in Australia (Boyd,
      1993)

e.   NA7201-7477
      A history of domestic architecture in
      Wagga Wagga, Australia (Johnson,
      1989)

f. HN101-942.5
A social history of mass media in Italy
(Romano, 1983)

g. HN101-942.5
Social reform literature in Finland in the
post World War II period (Trathen, 1978)

h. HV4761-4890.7
Animal rights in Aardt, Norway
(Sorenson, 1997)

i. B2750-2799
Criticism and interpretation of the
philospher, Immanuel Kant (Fuchs,
1996)

Biography Table

This section deals with the general principles and application of the Biography Table. More details and examples are in the *Subject Cataloging Manual. Shelflisting.*

For biographies about people who are not associated with any particular field, use the C schedule, particularly CT. For biographies about people in a particular field—e.g., music, paleontology—use that class or subject.

Some schedules—e.g., N and B—contain their own specific biography tables in the back of the schedule.

In Chapter 4, we dealt with specific biography instructions in the schedules for collective and individual biographies. Individual biographies are further subarranged using the Biography Table:

.x	Cutter for the biographee
.xA2	Collected works. By date.
.xA25	Selected works. Selections. By date
	Including quotations
.xA3	Autobiography, diaries, etc. By date
.xA4	Letters. By date
.xA5	Speeches, essays, and lectures. By date
	Including interviews
.xA6-Z	Individual biography, interviews, and criticism.
	By main entry
	Including criticism of selected works,
	autobiography, quotations, letters,
	speeches, interviews, etc.

Note the types of material in the Biography Table that require an additional cutter—e.g., Selected works, Autobiography, diaries, etc., Letters.

Example 1: Collective Biography
The lives of ten well-known Germans of the 19th century (Kessler, 1995):

D D	Germany
205	Biography and memoirs—19th-century history
.A2	Collective
.K47	main entry cutter
1995	date of publication

In this example, the cutter .A2 is an instruction in the schedule, and acts as a shelving cutter to bring together all collective biographies in 19th-century German history.

Example 2: Individual Biography (following instructions in schedule)
A biography of Hecker (Freitag, 1998):

D D	Germany
205	Biography and memoirs—19th-century history
.H37	Individual cutter within range .A3-Z, Hecker
.F74	main entry cutter for the author, Freitag
1998	date of publication

In this example, the instructions are in the schedule. The "individual" refers to the person about whom the biography is written. The individual must be cuttered within .A3-Z and is followed by a main entry cutter.

Example 3: Individual Biography for "Selected Works" (requiring Biography Table)

The subject of the book is the selected works of Ludwig Windthorst (1991):

D D	Germany
205	Biography and memoirs—19th-century history
.W4	Individual cutter within range .A3-Z, Windthorst
<u>.A25</u>	cutter from Biography Table for "Selected works" by date
1991	date of publication

We use .A25 from the Biography Table to bring together all selected works by Windthorst, arranged by date of publication.

Example 4: Individual Biography for "Letters" (requiring Biography Table)

This book contains Ludwig Windthorst's correspondence (1995):

D D	Germany
205	Biography and memoirs—19th-century history
.W4	Individual cutter, Windthorst
<u>.A4</u>	cutter from Biography Table for "Letters" by date
1995	date of publication

EXERCISE 5.15

Build complete call numbers for the following titles, using instructions in the schedules and the Biography Table when required. The author and the date of publication are in parentheses.

a. Albert Einstein: a biography (Folsing, 1997)

b. The love letters of Albert Einstein (Christie
    International Inc., 1996)

c. Media, consciousness and culture:
    explorations of Walter Ong's thought
    (edited by Gronbeck, 1991)

d. The magic lantern: an autobiography
    (Bergman, 1988)
    (Hint: Bergman is Ingmar Bergman, the film
    director.)

e. Colonel Elmer Ellsworth: a biography of the
    Civil War hero (Randall, 1960)

f. The rich men: a biography of millionaires in
    France (Sulitzer, 1991)

g. California biographical dictionary (1994)

h. Economists in Andalusia, Spain: a historical
    study (Soriano Diaz, 1990)
    (Hint: Subject is economic theory.)

i.   Setting the record straight: baseball's greatest batters (Grimble, 1998)

j.   Zero tollerance: an intimate memoir by the man who revolutionized figure skating (Cranston, 1997)

k.   Teilhard de Chardin: a biographical portrait of a paleontologist (Fatur, 1991)

Translation Table

This table is used across all schedules, except when specific instructions are provided for translations.

The classifier creates a cutter number for the original work, and expands it for the language of the translation according to the following table:

.x	Original works
.x12	Polyglot
.x13	English translation
.x14	French translation
.x15	German translation
.x16	Italian translation
.x17	Russian translation
.x18	Spanish translation

The Translation Table is used to cutter for a translation:
• when a uniform title and a language are provided and
• when the main entry is a personal author or title.

Translations generally follow the original work in alphabetical order by language.

For example, the original work *A brief history of time* by Stephen Hawking would be classified as follows:

QB	Astronomy
981	General works, treatises, etc. on Cosmogony. Cosmology
.H39	cutter for author, Hawking
1988	date of publication

The French translation of this work (translated by Leroux, published in 1995) would be:

QB	Astronomy
981	General works, treatises, etc. on Cosmogony. Cosmology
.H39<u>14</u>	cutter for author, Hawking + 14 for French translation
1995	date of publication

For translations in languages other than those specified in the Translation Table, create the language cutter.
- Use the Translation Table as the starting point.
- Fit the new number into the alphabetical sequence of translations of that work already in your collection.

For example, if your library already has a French and German translation of a work and you acquire a Hebrew translation, use .x16 for Hebrew. If later you acquire an Italian translation, use .x17 for Italian.

EXERCISE 5.16

Build a complete call number for the following works, using either the Translation Table or specific instructions in the schedules. The author, date of publication, and translation information are in parentheses.

a. The child's concept of physical causality (Piaget, 1970) (Italian translation by Salcito, 1986)

BF	
723	

b. An introduction to Feng Shui (Rossbach, 1985) (German translation by Valerius, 1995)

c. A sermon on religious charity (Sydney Smith, 1825) (German translation by Krogh, 1850)

d. A handbook on software engineering (Cockerill, 1991) (French translation by Masson, 1993)

e. Encyclopedia of birds (Hitchcock, 1979) (Russian translation by Grigorovich, 1985)

f. Don Quixote (Cervantes) (English translation for children, 1955)

g. Don Quixote (Cervantes) (French abridged translation by Tanti, 1935)

BF
B 1611
QA 76
QL
PQ 6323+
PQ 6323+

Language and Literature Tables

All the tables for classes P-PZ are in this one volume. The examples and exercises have been constructed using the 1982 edition of the *Language and Literature Tables*. In the new edition (1998) and in *Classification Plus*, the principles and application remain the same.

The answers are also the same regardless of which edition is used. However, the new edition may express the notation in a different but equivalent format, e.g., .Z5A3-39 (old edition), 0.Z5A3-Z5A39 (new edition).

If you are using the new editions of P classes and the *Language and Literature Tables*, translate the Roman numerals referred to in this workbook into Arabic numerals, e.g., XXXIX = 39, XL = 40.

EXERCISE 5.17

Use the P schedules and the *Language and Literature Tables* to answer these questions.

a. How do Tables P-PZ1 to P-PZ16 differ from Tables P-PZ20 to P-PZ50?

b. For the Flemish language, what Table would you use?
    (Hint: Use the PB-PH schedule.)

c. Using the table for the Flemish language, write down the number that appears in the Table for a general work on spoken language.

d. What Table or Tables would you use for the author, Cynthia Freeman?
    (Hint: Look in PS American Literature, Individual authors 1961-.)

e. How is the cutter for Freeman determined?
    (Hint: Read the instructions at the beginning of American Literature, Individual authors, 1900-1960 or 1961-.)

f. In Table XXXIX, what is the instruction for arrangement of collected plays?

g. In Table XXXIX, what is the instruction for arrangement and cuttering of general works of biography and criticism?

h.   In Table XL, what is the instruction for arrangement and cuttering of an autobiography?

Example 1

Let's say we have a work of fiction, *The Tommyknockers* (King, 1988):

American Literature
    Individual authors
        1961- (XXXIX or XL, unless otherwise specified)

PS	American Literature, Individual authors, 1961-
3561	authors starting with K
.I483	cutter based on second letter of surname, K<u>i</u>ng
.T66	cutter from Table XL for Separate works
1988	date of publication

The instruction in the schedule is to use either Table XXXIX or XL. In the *Language and Literature Tables*, Table XXXIX is for authors with one number, and Table XL is for authors with a cutter number. The above example is for an author with a cutter number—PS3561.I483—so we used Table XL. The instruction in Table XL—.xA61-Z458—is to cutter separate works by title, starting at .A61 and ending at .Z458.

Example 2

Let's say we have a general work of criticism and interpretation about Louis Zukofsky titled *Louis Zukofsky: a critical analysis* (Stewart, 1998):

> American Literature
>   Individual authors
>   1900-1960 (XL, unless otherwise specified)
>
> PS   American Literature, Individual authors, 1900-1960
> 3549   authors starting with Z
> .U47   cutter based on second letter of surname, Z**u**kofsky
> .Z87   cutter from Table XL for Biography and Criticism
> 1998   date of publication

The .Z87 cutter is determined in the following way:

1. Go to Table XL (the heading at the top of the page in the schedules tells you to use Table XL for further subarrangement "unless otherwise specified")

2. Find the section on Biography and criticism

3. Note that the instruction in this section for General works is <u>.xZ5-999</u>

4. This means that:

    - .x = author cutter for Zukofsky, so .x = <u>.U47</u>

    - the main entry must start with <u>.Z</u>

    - the main entry cannot start before <u>.Z5</u>

    - all main entries (whichever letter they start with) must be fitted in between .Z5-Z999

5. Stewart is the main entry in the above example, so:

    - <u>S</u>, towards the end of the alphabet, will be near the end of the 5-999 range, so S = 8

    - the second letter of S**t**ewart is cuttered according to paragraph (2) of the LC Cutter Table, so t = 7

    - Stewart = <u>.Z87</u> (your final cutter will depend on your shelflist)

EXERCISE 5.18

Use the Language and Literature Table XL and the author Zukofsky to build a complete call number.

a. Upper limit music: the writing of Louis Zukofsky (edited by Scroggins, 1997)

b. Louis Zukofsky and the transformation of a
    modern American poetics (Stanley, 1994)

c. Collected fiction (Zukofsky, 1990)

d. The selected works of Louis Zukofsky
    (edited by Creeley, 1991)

e. Prepositions: the collected critical essays of
    Louis Zukofsky (Zukofsky, 1981)

EXERCISE 5.19

Use the *Language and Literature Tables* and the schedule for Literature (General), English and American
Literature. Build a complete call number. The author and the date of publication are in parentheses.

a. Memoirs of Virginia Woolf (edited by Lee,
    1997)

b. The letters of Nancy Mitford and Evelyn
    Waugh (edited by Mosley, 1996)

c. The symbolism of Nathaniel Parker Willis
(Hawthorne, 1951)
(Hint: Look in 19th-century American
Literature.)

d. She loved roses (T. A. Ismail, 1990)
(Hint: This is a novel by an Egyptian author
who writes in English. Look at PR9375.)

e. Gore Vidal: a critical companion (Baker,
1997)

f. The diaries and memoirs of Samuel Taylor
Coleridge (edited by Crittenden, 1987)
(Hint: Look in 19th-century English
Literature.)

g. The collected works of Sabine Baring-Gould
(edited by Alderman, 1992)
(Hint: Look in 19th-century English
Literature.)

h. My brilliant career (Franklin, 1902)
(Hint: Look at English Literature outside of
Great Britain - Australia PR9619.3.)

i. The dramatization of the poems of John
Greenleaf Whittier (Green, 1988)
(Hint: Look in 19th-century American
Literature.)

j. Primary colors: a novel of politics
    (Anonymous, 1996)
    (Hint: Use "Anonymous works" in
    American Literature 1961-.)

k. On the other side of the rainbow: the
    autobiography of Dinker Dawg (1997)
    (Hint: This is an autobiography of a dog.)

l. An autobiography (Frame, 1991)
    (Hint: Look at English Literature outside of
    Great Britain - New Zealand PR9639.3.)

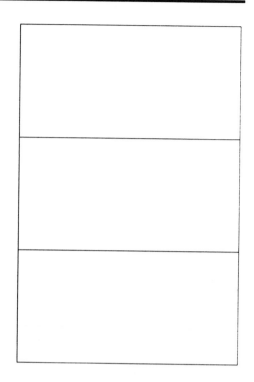

Chapter 6
SHELVING

Shelving Procedure

When shelving, read the LCC call number on the spine label **line by line.** You only need to look at the second line if the letters and/or numbers on the first line are the same, and so on.

1. Shelve letters alphabetically by class or subclass. Single letters will come at the beginning of each sequence:

D, DD, DJK, L, LB, LC, M, N, NA, NK, P, PA, etc.

2. Shelve the number immediately following the letter or letters as a whole number:

LB	LB	LB	LB
15	775	1028	3497

3. Shelve numbers preceded by a decimal point as decimal numbers:

LB	LB	LB	LB
3621	3621	3621	3621
.25	.3	.5	.65

4. Shelve cutter numbers alphabetically, then as decimal numbers:

LB	LB	LB	LB
3621	3621	3621	3621
.3	.3	.3	.3
.A252	.A32	.C3342	.C42

5. Shelve class numbers with a cutter number before class numbers followed by a decimal number:

LC	LC	LC	LC
149	149	149	149
.D58	.H37	.5	.7
		.M67	.W55

6. Shelve call numbers with double cutters alphabetically by the first cutter, then, if the first cutter is the same, alphabetically by the second cutter:

LC 3501 .H38 .Q56	LC 3501 .M26 .B43	LC 3501 .M3 .T64	LC 3650 .I74 .D35	LC 3650 .I74 .E66

7. Different editions of the same work are distinguished by the date of publication and are shelved chronologically:

LB 14 .7 .P48 **1982**	LB 14 .7 .P48 **1989**	LB 14 .7 .P48 **1995**

8. Volume numbering on the spine label is often used to distinguish each volume in a multi-volume set if there is no distinct numbering already on the spine:

LA 134 .C66 1992 **v.1**	LA 134 .C66 1992 **v.2**	LA 134 .C66 1992 **v.3**

Spine Labeling

Call numbers are represented on a spine label in many different ways:

LC149 .D58 1995	LB3621 .3 .A32 1991	LC3650 .I74D35 1996	HB2508 .5 .S58U72 1970	HB 2508.5 S58 U72 1970

EXERCISE 6.1

Sort the following call numbers into correct shelf order.

QA 16 .M53 1996	QA 95 .A33 1986	QA 77 .B76 1994	QA 39 .S65 1990	QA 77 .F75 1983	QA 39 .S65 1987
QA 16 .D58 1979	QA 77 .F75 1989	QA 39 .S66 1988	QA 16 .M533 1994	QA 95 .A332 1975	QA 77 .B766 1978
QA 16 .G24 1986	QA 39 .S652 1989	QA 95 .A3312 1991			

Exercise 6.2

Sort the following call numbers into correct shelf order.

N 7432 .I86 1991	N 7431 .5 .A34 1990	N 7432 .3 .C64 1991	N 7432 .5 .A78 .K93 1982	N 7431 .Q562 1974	N 7431 .Q56 1990
N 7432 .5 .A2 .J86 1994	N 7431 .5 .A34 1996	N 7431 .Q563 1989	N 7432 .3 .D76 1995	N 7431 .P47 1973	N 7431 .5 .A34 1986

EXERCISE 6.3

Sort the following call numbers into correct shelf order.

BF 175 .5 .D44 .Q36 1993	BF 175 .5 .D44 .C66 1993	BF 175 .5 .D74 .W45 1994	BF 175 .5 .M37 .F76 1996	BF 175 .5 .D74 .W45 1990
BF 175 .5 .A72 .P43 1989	BF 175 .5 .I43 .P76 1987	BF 175 .5 .E35 .B53 1993	BF 175 .5 .K45 .K87 1995	BF 175 .5 .M37 .F76 1994

EXERCISE 6.4

Sort the following call numbers into correct shelf order.

BD431 .M897 1952	BH301 .M54F75 1985	B831 .2 .N38 1997	BF1040 .B255 1992	BF109 .J8M34 1996
BH301 .M54P67 1985	BD431 .K58 1991	BF1040 .B25 1993	BH301 .M54P67 1988	BF109 .J8S74 1994
B831 .2 .N66 1993	BF1040 .B35 1990	BD431 .L43 1992	BF109 .J8N65 1994	

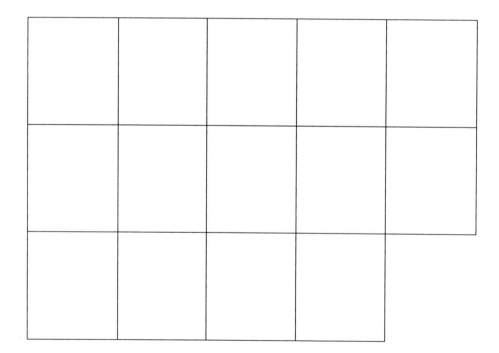

Chapter 7
CLASSIFICATION PLUS

Introduction

Classification Plus is an electronic version of the Library of Congress Classification schedules and the Library of Congress Subject Headings.

Classification Plus consists of a series of infobases. Separate infobases include the Welcome Screen, the Library of Congress Subject Headings, the classification schedules, the prefaces and the various external classification tables. You can move around the infobases through hypertext links. Each infobase is indexed so you can search for a single word, phrase or class number.

Advantages of *Classification Plus*

1. All catalogers have the most recent schedules.
2. Multiple users can simultaneously access the same information.
3. The schedules and the Library of Congress Subject Headings are linked in one product.
4. The ordering and management of classification schedules is simplified for libraries.

Disadvantages of *Classification Plus*

1. A complete set of schedules is not yet available.
2. The structure and format of the schedules are not obvious for first-time users; familiarity with the print version assists in understanding the structure of *Classification Plus*.
3. It is less conducive to browsing.
4. Catalogers spend more time doing computer-based work.

Searching *Classification Plus*

Classification Plus can be searched using:
- words
- phrases
- Boolean logic
- special templates designed for querying the infobases.

Obtaining a Demo of *Classification Plus*

A demonstration version of this product can be downloaded from the Library of Congress website: http://lcweb.loc.gov/cds. Follow the link to CD-ROM products.

The exercises in this chapter have been designed for the demonstration version.

Learning to Use *Classification Plus*

Begin by clicking on the "Help Topics" bar and then the "Basic introduction" icon for an overview of *Classification Plus*. Then we suggest that new users click on the "How do I ..." icon to step you through searching for information on *Classification Plus*.

EXERCISE 7.1

Select the H schedule. Click on the Query button on the toolbar at the bottom of the screen and search for the following words. Write down the number of hits you had for each search.

a. Medicine   _____

b. Strikes   _____

c. Recession   _____

d. Accounting   _____

e. Miners   _____

f. Energy   _____

g. Construction   _____

EXERCISE 7.2

Use the Query button and find the class number for the following.

a. Sympathetic strikes   _____

b. Rehabilitation counseling   _____

c. Guaranteed annual wage   _____

d. Women college graduates   _____

e. Corporate image   _____

EXERCISE 7.3

Go to the HF subclass. Follow the instructions and answer the questions.

a.   Click on the hyperlink HF294+ at the beginning of the HF subclass. What is the class number for General works on boards of trade?

b.   Use the back arrow on the toolbar at the top of the screen to go back to the beginning of HF. Click on HF3000+. What is the caption at HF3003?

c.   Use the scroll bar and scroll down to HF5473.A3-Z. Click on the hypertext link. What can you do at this table?

d.   Look at the Reference Window pane (the white window above the schedule listing). How many captions are there? List the last two captions.

EXERCISE 7.4

Select Query Template 1 from the toolbar at the bottom of the screen and search for the following class numbers or caption keywords. Write down the caption or class number.

a.   HF1111   _____

b.   HF1428   _____

c.   HF3041   _____

d.   HF5382   _____

e.   HF5413   _____

f.   Direct marketing   _____

g.   Complaint letters   _____

h.   Business translating   _____

EXERCISE 7.5

Use the Advanced Query Template to answer the following questions.

a. Do a word search on alcohol. How many hits do you get? Click OK to go into the schedules.

b. Click on the next hit arrow on the toolbar at the bottom of the screen to find the class number for alcohol fuel. What is the class number?

c. Do a word search on labor. How many hits do you get? Click OK to go into the schedules.

d. Click on the next hit arrow on the toolbar at the bottom of the screen to find the class number for labor bureaus. What is the class number?

e. Click on the hyperlink for labor bureaus in the United States. What is the caption at HD8055.A-Z?

EXERCISE 7.6

Select any one of the query options and find the class number for General works for the following terms.

a. Refuse disposal   _____

b. Overtime   _____

c. Work sharing   _____

d. Contracting   _____

e. Cottage industries   _____

EXERCISE 7.7

Use the appropriate query template and search for the class number HD4001-4420.7.

a. What is the caption at that range of numbers?   _____

b. What Table are you referred to?   _____

c. What is the base number?   _____

d. What is the class number for Tunisia?   _____

e. If you have a work about the city of Tunis in Tunisia (Akbar, 1999), what will your call number be?

Chapter 8
MORE PRACTICE

EXERCISE 8.1

This exercise uses the KJ-KKZ Law of Europe schedule. Build complete call numbers for the following works. The author and the date of publication are in parentheses.

a. Marriage in Celtic law (Ferguson, 1961)

b. Civil service of the Benelux Economic Union (1979)

c. A general work on inheritance in Roman law (Aaronson, 1955)

d. Rules governing the official language of the European Free Trade Association (1990)

e. A general work on police and public safety in the city of Uppsala (Christensen, 1989)

EXERCISE 8.2

This exercise uses the K Law (General) schedule. Build complete call numbers for the following works. The author and the date of publication are in parentheses.

a. The teaching of taxation law (Boal, 1989)

b. International Conference on Equity and Fairness in Law (5th : 1985 : Geneva) Proceedings (1986)

c. A casebook on comparative family law (Zimmerman, 1981)

d. The problem of pornography: regulation and the right to free speech (Easton, 1994)

e. The law of war crimes: national and international approaches (edited by McCormack, 1997)

f. Corporate and commercial law: modern developments (edited by Feldman, 1996)

g. Permissible killing: the self-defense justification of homicide (Uniacke, 1994)

EXERCISE 8.3

This exercise is based on the N schedule. Answer the following questions.

a.   In the NA subclass, name the range of class numbers for "Architecture of special countries".

b.   Which table are you referred to for the country number?

c.   What is the base number for calculating your country number?

d.   How should you read the note for "Special artists" in the instructions?

e.   Find the caption and number for "Special artists" in Table 5 for Mexico and add this number to the base number.

f.   In the sculpture subclass, find the range of class numbers at "Special countries".

g.   In the NC subclass, find the range of class numbers at "Special countries".

h.   In what parts of the schedule would you use Table N6?

i.   In Table N6, what does the first cutter designate?

j.   Is Table N7 used throughout the schedule?

k.   Use the index and find the entries for Frank Lloyd Wright, J. M. W. Turner, Jackson Pollock and Monet Are there entries?

EXERCISE 8.4

This exercise is based on the N schedule. Find the call number for the following works. The author and the date of publication are in parentheses. Use these steps:

1. Determine the media.
2. Determine the country number by using the range of class numbers at "Special countries" and the relevant table.
3. Cutter the artist and then subarrange using Table N6 or N7 unless otherwise specified.

a. A critical review of Jackson Pollock's sketchbooks (Pedvin, 1997)

b. Jackson Pollock: the painter (Ackerman, 1998)

c. The architecture of Frank Lloyd Wright (Pfeiffer, 1993)

d. Edward Cullinan Architects: a firm's contribution to English architecture (Rowbottom, 1989)

e. Henry Moore: letters by an English sculptor (edited by Josephson, 1987)

f. Alvar Aalto: the life of a Finnish furniture designer (Wynne-Ellis, 1985)

g. Alvar Aalto: his architectural legacy
    (Mangone, 1993)

h. Glenn Murcutt: a pioneer of an Australian
    architectural form (Bond, 1985)

i. Italian illuminations (Alexander, 1977)

EXERCISE 8.5

This exercise focuses on expanding the second cutter. Build complete call numbers for the following titles at the indicated class numbers. The author and the date of publication are in parentheses.

a. Broom makers in Louisiana (McIntosh,
    1991)

| HD |
| 8039 |

b. The stainless steel industry in Pittsburgh: a
    history of growth (Sherman, 1982)

| HD |
| 9529 |

c. The General Motors Corporation: future
    challenges in the automobile industry
    (Donner, 1967)

| HD |
| 9710 |

d. The Garden of Shah Jehan in India (Lal, 1970)	SB 466
e. Fox hunting in Kent, England (Roberts, 1972)	S K 287

EXERCISE 8.6

This exercise uses tables. Use the H schedule and build complete call numbers. The author and the date of publication are in parentheses.

a. Privilege in the Soviet Union: a study of the elite under communism (Dubrowski, 1978)	
b. Social indicators for Ethiopia (Tuksar, 1968)	
c. Municipal finance in Dominica: public debt problems (Marques, 1993)	
d. Customs administration in the Czech Republic: the smuggling issue (Riszko, 1998)	

e.   Illegal gangs in Ontario (Lamb, 1976)

f.   Lotteries in Malaysia (Mudin, 1990)

g.   Postwar land use policy in Papua New
Guinea (McCarthy, 1982)

h.   Communism in Eastern Europe (Schopflin,
1993)

i.   Antonio Gramsci: biography of an Italian
communist (Holub, 1992)

j.   Prisons in Bangkok, Thailand (Lim, 1995)

EXERCISE 8.7

This exercise requires you to build complete call numbers with dates as part of the class numbers. The author and the date of publication are in parentheses.

a. British coal miners strike, 1984-85
    (Sawbridge, 1990)

b. The Cananea Consolidated Copper
    Company strike in Mexico in 1906 (Meyer,
    1980)

c. The causes of the 1929 stock market crash
    (Bierman, 1998) (Hint: Look under economic
    crises.)

d. Endangered dreams: the Great Depression
    of 1929 in California (Starr, 1996)

e. The economic crisis of 1857 in Hamburg,
    Germany (Ahrens, 1986)

f. The myth of the British Great Depression
    1873-1896 (Saul, 1969)

g. Official report of the Games of the XXIIIrd
    Olympiad, Los Angeles, 1984 (main entry is
    Olympic Games (23rd : 1984 : Los Angeles,
    Calif.))

h.   The Nazi Olympics of 1936 (Mandell, 1987)

i.   Olympics 2000: and the winner is? (Sydney Organising Committee for the Olympic Games, 1999)

EXERCISE 8.8

Put the call numbers from Exercise 8.7 into correct shelf order.

a.   _____

b.   _____

c.   _____

d.   _____

e.   _____

f.   _____

g.   _____

h.   _____

i.   _____

EXERCISE 8.9

Adjust the following cutter numbers (from MARC records) in the shelflist to two digits whenever possible. Some numbers cannot be reduced without losing vital information, e.g., translations. The main entry word is provided for each call number.

a.   HD58.8.C655 1988   Contemporary   _____

b.   HD58.8.C658 1990   Corporate   _____

c.   HD58.8.D862 1990   Dunphy   _____

d.   HD58.8.H363 1989   Hannan   _____

e.   HD58.8.H3633 1994   Hardy, C.
                                     Managing   _____

f.   HD58.8.H364 1990   Hardy, C.
                                     Strategies   _____

g.   HD58.8.H365 1988   Harrigan   _____

h.   HD58.8.M32513 1993   Mastenbroek   _____

i.   HD58.82.M3698 1999   Marquardt   _____

j.   ND1495.P8.G3713 1993   Garau   _____

k.   PR6043.O78.G39818 1983   Taratuta   _____

l.   TR146.M628 1982   Morley   _____

m.   TR653.R46313 1998   Renger-Patzsch   _____

n.   TR681.F3.K3742 1996   Karsh   _____

ANSWERS

EXERCISE 1.1

Supermarkets	by type of product, fresh food, frozen food, confectionery, pet food, etc.
Employees	by salary, duties, qualifications, status, etc.
Schools	by age, ability, gender, denomination, etc.
Mail	by country, city, zip code, airmail, sea mail, etc.
Personal papers	by year, financial, correspondence, recipes, family member, work-related, etc.

EXERCISE 1.2

a. To order the fields of knowledge in a systematic way, to bring related items together in a helpful sequence, to provide orderly access to the shelves either by browsing or via the catalog.

b. Enumerative classification attempts to spell out all the single and composite subject concepts required. Examples include the Library of Congress Classification and, to a lesser extent, the Dewey Decimal Classification.

   Synthetic classification lists numbers for single concepts and numbers are constructed for composite subjects. Examples include the Colon Classification, the Universal Decimal Classification and some features of the Dewey Decimal Classification.

c. Classification schedules are arranged by subject.

d. Number building is the ability of the scheme to allow the construction of notation to include items not specifically mentioned in the schedules. It is a desirable feature because no schedule can be entirely enumerative and new topics, subjects, and geographic areas are continually being added.

e. Hierarchical classification is based on the division of subjects from the most general to the most specific.

f. A library should consider the nature of its client group when it classifies its material so that policies and procedures are useful and suitable to its users' needs.

EXERCISE 2.1

a. It was developed because the previous system was no longer adequate for the collection.
b. Each schedule has an index. However, there is no one overall index to all the schedules.
c. Alphanumeric notation means that the notation is a mixture of letters and numbers.
d. You need to determine the subject.
e. There are 43 schedules.

f. 1. NA7105.D58 1997   or   NA
                                 7105
                                 .D58
                                 1997

    2. PS   or   PS3525   or   PS3525.E6645.A6 1997
        3525   .E6645
        .E6645   .A6
        .A6   1997
        1997

    3. LC   or   LC929
        929   .3
        .3   .T5
        .T5   .B35
        .B35   1982
        1982

EXERCISE 3.1

a. Military science   U
b. Religion   B
c. Science   Q
d. Education   L
e. Law   K
f. Librarianship   Z
g. Geography   G

EXERCISE 3.2

a. Wartime submarines   V
b. Encyclopaedia Britannica   A
c. Public libraries   Z
d. Treatment of cancer   R
e. Landscape painting   N
f. Astronomy for beginners   Q
g. Growing orchids   S
h. Teaching adults   L
i. Defense in the modern world   U
j. History of jazz   M
k. Designing buildings   N
l. Federal government administration   J
m. Voyages of Christopher Columbus   G
n. The American legal system   K
o. Bridge engineering   T
p. Biblical studies   B
q. The Japanese economy   H
r. The plays of William Shakespeare   P
s. The American Civil War   C-F

EXERCISE 3.3

a.	Secret societies	HS
b.	Communism	HX
c.	Statistics	HA
d.	Marriage	HQ
e.	Transport	HE

EXERCISE 3.4

a.	World banking	HG
b.	Violence in the home	HQ
c.	The future of speed rail	HE
d.	Encyclopedia of sociology	HM
e.	Readings on international trade	HF
f.	Statistical dictionary	HA
g.	The caste system in India	HT
h.	Government income and expenditure	HJ
i.	Social science methodology	H
j.	Origins of the Boy Scout movement	HS
k.	Population projections for the year 2000	HB
l.	Development of social movements in Canada	HN
m.	Sociology of crime	HV
n.	Readings in Marxist philosophy	HX
o.	The American economy	HC or HD
p.	Origins of modern social theory	H

EXERCISE 3.5

C	Auxiliary Sciences of History
D-DJ	History (General), History of Europe. Part 1.
DJK-DK	History of Eastern Europe: General, Soviet Union, Poland
DL-DR	History of Europe. Part 2.
DS-DX	History of Asia, Africa, Australia, New Zealand, etc.
E-F	History: America

EXERCISE 3.6

a.	A book of Russian poetry	PG
b.	A history of Australia	DS-DX
c.	Manual of geology	Q
d.	Henry Moore's sculpture	N
e.	Guide to camping	G
f.	Canadian law	KE
g.	Pediatrics	R
h.	Woodwind instruments	M

EXERCISE 3.7

a. Periodicals, societies, congresses, serial collections, yearbooks
b. Dictionaries and encyclopedias
c. General works (Note that this is indented under History)
d. General works, treatises, and textbooks

e.   Special aspects of the subject as a whole, A-Z
f.   Economic ecology

EXERCISE 3.8

a.   An ecology journal   QH540
b.   Philosophy of ecology   QH540.5
c.   A general work on the history of ecology   QH540.8
d.   General textbooks on ecology   QH541
e.   Tables and formulas for ecologists   QH541.142
f.   A book on chemical ecology   QH541.15.C44
g.   A book on landscape ecology   QH541.15.L35

EXERCISE 3.9

a.   CR4509
b.   CR4513
c.   CR4485.C7
d.   CR4505
e.   CR4480

EXERCISE 3.10

a.   Confer notes   Cf. SB115, Seed and plant catalogs
                           Cf. SB118.48+, Nurseries

b.   See notes   For works limited to a specific plant, see the plant, e.g. SB409, Orchids; SB411, Roses
                           For works on general plant propagation, see SB119+
                           Biography, see SB61+
                           For works limited to special plants, see the plant, e.g. SB406.7-83, Flowers; SB419,
                               House plants

c.   Apply table at note   SB118.74.A-Z
                               Apply table at SB85.A-Z

d.   Including notes   Seed treatment
                               Including irradiation, stratification, etc.
                           Preservation. Protection
                               Including seed deterioration
                           Synthetic seeds
                               Including somatic embryogenesis

EXERCISE 3.11

a.   RC918.M8
b.   RC901.7.A7
c.   Kidney, Artificial: RC901.7.A7
d.   General works
e.   NC1764+
f.   General works (Note that the class number in the index for computer art is N7433.8+. The "+" sign indicates
     that there are subtopics at that class number in the schedule.)

g. Periodicals and societies (Note that the class number in the index is NB1+; in this case, the "+" refers to the whole subclass.)
h. Yes (Note that there is an entry in the index also under Doodles.)
i. No (Synonyms for graffiti such as street art, spray-can art, public art did not give us a class number. A classifier will need to look further for the best place in the schedules.)

EXERCISE 3.12

		Schedule	Class number
a.	Cancer research	R	RC267
b.	Japanese gardens	S	SB458
c.	General work on forest fires	S	SD421
d.	A bibliography on bookbinding	Z	Z266.5
e.	Clay pot cookery	T	TX825.5
f.	An accounting dictionary	H	HF5621
g.	Breeding Siberian huskies	S	SF429.S65
h.	Keynesian economics	H	HB99.7
i.	Making Christmas decorations	T	TT900.C4
j.	History of osteopathy	R	RZ321
k.	Preserving cherries	T	TX612.C5
l.	Nursing in Australia	R	RT15
m.	Women landscape architects	S	SB469.375
n.	History of geometry	Q	QA443.5
o.	The OCLC library network	Z	Z674.82.O15
p.	Manual for a Yashica camera	T	TR263.Y3
q.	Bonsai gardens	S	SB433.5
r.	The solar system for children	Q	QB501.3
s.	The adventures of Charles Darwin, the naturalist	Q	QH31.D2

EXERCISE 4.1

The following numbers and captions should be highlighted:
76.7   General works
76.73.C25   COBOL

EXERCISE 4.2

a. QA Mathematics
b. QA76.5
c. QA76.57.D44
d. QA76.6
e. QA76.73.B3

EXERCISE 4.3

a. 1. E462
   2. F73.18
   3. ND1489
   4. SF515.5.S64
   5. PN1992.7
b. #2, #4 and #5

c. 1. .O̱28 (see Note)
   2. .H58
   3. .C65
   4. .M33
   5. .B75
d. 1. .O28 1998
   2. .H58 1995
   3. .C65 1997
   4. .M33 1991
   5. .B75 1995

Note: A small dash may be used under the letter "O̱" to distinguish it from the digit zero. This is useful for spine labels.

EXERCISE 4.4

a. PA2259
b. P98.3
c. B398.G65
d. BF105
e. HQ799.2.M35
f. HB3717
g. GV1047.W3
h. GV722
i. DL326
j. DR66.6

EXERCISE 4.5

a.	Appiah	.A67
b.	Brettell	.B74
c.	O'Reilly	.O74
d.	Cousineau	.C68
e.	Schonell	.S36
f.	Takagi	.T35
g.	Dasgupta	.D37
h.	D'Ambrosio	.D36
i.	Rubin	.R83
j.	Wang	.W36
k.	Dukic	.D85
l.	Sanchez	.S26
m.	Quinlan	.Q56
n.	Papadopoulos	.P37
o.	Isfahani	.I84
p.	Beauchamps	.B43
q.	Somare	.S66
r.	Urquhart	.U77
s.	Fagyas	.F34
t.	Tippet	.T57
u.	Halupka	.H35
v.	Li	.L5
w.	Smith	.S65

EXERCISE 4.6

a.   Leaders and managers   .L43
b.   Between the earthquakes   .B48
c.   Qualitative evaluation methods   .Q35
d.   Emergence of a free press   .E44
e.   Out of Africa   .O98
f.   Social anthropology   .S63
g.   Interviewing skills   .I58
h.   Quince novelas hispanoamericanas   .Q56
i.   Sept ans chez les hommes libres   .S47
j.   Education and political development   .E38
k.   Principles and practices of infectious diseases   .P75
l.   Composing an opera   .C66
m.   Industrialization and culture   .I53
n.   Algebraic theory of semigroups   .A44
o.   Undersea lightwave communications   .U53
p.   Jurassic Park   .J87

EXERCISE 4.7

a.   World Bank   .W67
b.   Universal Studios   .U55
c.   British Broadcasting Corporation   .B75
d.   Mambo   .M36
e.   United States. Congress. Committee on Armed Services .U55
f.   Qantas Airways   .Q26

EXERCISE 4.8

a.   El Greco   .E44
b.   St. Augustine   .S73
c.   MacIntosh   .M33
d.   Dal Santo   .D35
e.   McManus   .M36 or .M46
f.   Saint Agnes   .S25
g.   Le Mesurier   .L46
h.   An acoustic experience   .A26 or .A36
i.   De Souza   .D47
j.   Los jardines de Granada   .J37
k.   McKenzie-Clay   .M35 or .M45

EXERCISE 4.9

a.   1993
b.   1990
c.   1993
d.   1997
e.   1978
f.   1985
g.   1990z
h.   1994
i.   1997

j.   1988
k.   1900z
l.   1982
m.   1978
n.   1983
o.   1970z

EXERCISE 4.10

a.   F
     73
     .18
     .R84
     1997

b.   NK
     1173
     .M37
     1998

c.   TA
     166
     .E74
     1992
     (Note 1)

d.   TA
     166
     .E74
     1997
     (Note 1)

e.   RA
     427
     .5
     .J33
     1995

f.   MT
     7
     .E44
     1995
     (Note 2)

g.   AM
     7
     .T49
     1986

h.   G
     154
     .9
     .W67
     1997

i.   TR
     642
     .K69
     1986

j.   TR
     642
     .K69
     1990

k.   E
     76
     .2
     .D53
     1972

l.   CS
     88
     .N8
     .G46
     1990

m.   TR
     154
     .I58
     1994

n.   E
     456
     .A44
     1996
     (Note 2)

o.   NK
     1174
     .I58
     1993

Note 1: Use the date of the conference, not the date of publication.
Note 2: The title is the main entry when a work is edited.

EXERCISE 4.11

a.   NK
     1170
     .E28
     1996

b.   NK
     1170
     .C37
     1994

c.   NK
     1170
     .B94
     1995

d.   NK
     1170
     .C68
     1985

e.   NK
     1170
     .D47
     1989

f.   NK
     1170
     .G74
     1982

g.   NK
     1170
     .D47
     1990

h.   NK
     1170
     .C86
     1984

i.   NK
     1170
     .D47
     1987

EXERCISE 4.12

Your cutter numbers may be slightly different from those in the answers. This is fine as long as you have left some space for new works.

a.   NK1170.B87 1990   Business
b.   NK1170.B94 1995   Byers
c.   NK1170.C37 1994   Cargill
d.   NK1170.C66 1985   Council for Design
e.   NK1170.C68 1979   Council for National Academic Awards
f.   NK1170.C73 1990   Cranbrook design discourse
g.   NK1170.C86 1984   Cunningham

h.	NK1170.D47 1987	Design and aesthetics
i.	NK1170.D48 1989	Design and art education in schools (Note 1)
j.	NK1170.D49 1987	Design Education Symposium (Note 1)
k.	NK1170.D52 1990	Design italiano (Note 1)
l.	NK1170.D63 1978	Dodd
m.	NK1170.E28 1996	Eaton
n.	NK1170.E34 1976	Eggleston
o.	NK1170.G74 1974	Great Britain
p.	NK1170.G75 1974	Green, Petra (Note 2)
q.	NK1170.G76 1982	Green, Roger
r.	NK1170.M35 1977	Maier
s.	NK1170.M35 1980	Maier

Note 1: You could use three digits for your cutter numbers, e.g., i) .D473, j) .D476 and k) .D478.

Note 2: Cutter numbers at p and q—.G75 and .G76—are close but it is unlikely that there will be many more authors with a first name starting with "p" or "r". There is enough space for expansion to a third digit.

EXERCISE 4.13

a. BF455.D363 1982
b. BF455.D364 1982
c. BF455.D365 1969
d. BF455.D366 1973
e. BF455.D367 1991
f. BF455.D368 1976

EXERCISE 4.14

Your cutter numbers may be slightly different from those in the answers.

a. .M33
b. .M34
c. .M35
d. .M36
e. .M37
f. .M44
g. .M442
h. .M445
i. .M45
j. .M46
k. .M47

EXERCISE 4.15

a. LB	b. LC	c. LC	d. LB	e. RG
1140	51	586	1780	696
.A18	.T57	.A45	.V36	.C87
.S65	1994	.E75	1993	1998
1997		1992		

f.	RC	g.	RD	h.	RC	i.	Z	j.	Z
	373		145		313		144		682
	.A53		.X53		.A57		.P47		.25
	1990		1986		.U53		1985		.F47
					1989				1994

k.	Z	l.	ZA	m.	QR	n.	QE	o.	QH
	679		3205		201		501		541
	.57		.D53		.T53		.4		.5
	.T63		1999		.H37		.N9		.M27
	1989				1994		.R83		.C85
							1991		1995

EXERCISE 4.16

a.	PR	b.	PR	c.	PR	d.	PR	e.	PR
	6037		6037		6037		6037		6037
	.P29		.P29		.P29		.P29		.P29
	.P8		.B3		.G5		.F3		.P7
	1993		1990		1998		1988		1961

f.	PR	g.	PR	h.	PR	i.	PR
	6037		6037		6037		6037
	.P29		.P29		.P29		.P29
	.A2		.R4		.C6		.P7
	1995		1996		1994		1994

EXERCISE 4.17

a.	PR	b.	PR	c.	PR	d.	PR	e.	PR
	6037		6037		6037		6037		6037
	.P29		.P29		.P29		.P29		.P29
	.A2		.B3		.C6		.F3		.G5
	1995		1990		1994		1988		1998

f.	PR	g.	PR	h.	PR	i.	PR
	6037		6037		6037		6037
	.P29		.P29		.P29		.P29
	.P7		.P7		.P8		.R4
	1961		1994		1993		1996

EXERCISE 4.18

a. QA9.A1
b. QC883.7
c. TP890
d. TX165.A1
e. BF180
f. BF173.A2
g. BJ1188.5
h. B819.5.A1

EXERCISE 4.19

a. .A1
b. RA565.A2
c. RA565.A32 1994
d. #2
e. BF109.A1

EXERCISE 4.20

a.	SB	b.	SB	c.	SB	d.	SB	e.	SB
	470		470		470		470		470
	.54		.55		.55		.54		.55
	.O3		.I8		.E85		.P4		.D4
	.G74		.F66		.S74		.F85		.L86
	1992		1986		1990		1988		1995

f.	SB	g.	SB	h.	SB
	470		470		470
	.55		.55		.55
	.S72		.A8		.C29
	.L36		.T39		.D35
	1991		1987		1994

Note: The *Regions and Countries Table* and the table for *American States and Canadian Provinces* were used for the area cutters in this exercise.

EXERCISE 5.1

a. 3
b. Yes
c. No
d. QC45.A-Z
e. QC48
f. 36
g. Table of Economic Subdivisions (10 nos.)
h. H15 is for 10 nos., H16 is for 5 nos., H17 is for 1 no.
i. HS1701-1705
j. Yes
k. No
l. TA6.A2-Z
m. Yes
n. Yes
o. .x2A-Z
p. 14
q. Subarrangement for Exhibitions
r. Tables of Regions of Countries (1000 numbers)
s. Table N1, table at NK2813-2896.3
t. 3
u. Cities, A-Z
v. .x2A - .x2Z
w. LC573
x. LC571
y. 3 (This is an example of how some tables have been arranged in older schedules.)

EXERCISE 5.2

a. TJ
603
.4
.M4
.T56
1972

b. SF
243
.5
.V4
.C78
1983

c. HM
22
.F7
.G74
1991

d. N
5208
.I8
.S47
1994

e. NA
6862
.T5
.H35
1989

f. QD
47
.5
.I8
.S38
1996

g. RA
413
.5
.G7
.M33
1995

h. LB
3491
.A6
.U89
1981

EXERCISE 5.3

a. HG
1939
.S73
.M34
1997

b. LC
929
.3
.T52
.B35
1982

c. QD
2
.U62
.S25
1989

d. NA
7858
.F82
.P35
1985

e. NC
998
.6
.C62
.B47
1990

f. QK
480
.A82
.W39
1988

g. HF
5469
.23
.U63
.A83
1998

h. RA
523
.G82
.A83
1994

i. RA
630
.I54
.J33
1991

Note: Depending on the number of works in your library in particular subject areas, you may need to extend your main entry cutter by another digit or digits.

EXERCISE 5.4

a. LB
475
.C52
.P65
1990
(see Note)

b. HJ
5715
.C22
.Q37
1994

c. SF
83
.G73
.R67
1986

d. HF
5465
.U635
.N43
1992

e. QC
47
.C23
.U54
1995

f. BJ
2007
.J37
.S758
1984

Note: Did you notice the number for Cheever below the table?

EXERCISE 5.5

a.	LB	b.	N	c.	HB	d.	HV
	2803		7433		129		5831
	.2		.4		.H49		.M6
	.J3		.B73		.W55		.A63
	.A437		.Z74		1986		1999
	1991		1989				
			(see Note)				

Note: The range of numbers is limited to .Z7-.Z99. The letter "c" is near the beginning of the alphabet so it will have to be closer to 7 than to 9.

EXERCISE 5.6

a.	R	b.	R	c.	R	d.	R	e.	R
	473		546		534		498		608
	.H57		.A1		.A1		.6		.S56
	1985		.R49		.P67		.M85		.H86
			1994		1972		1984		1995
					(see Note)				

f.	R	g.	R	h.	R	i.	R	j.	R
	591		604		608		538		654
	.M33		.C58		.5		.A1		.A1
	1983		.T45		.A1		.K79		.D87
			1969		.W53		1990		1981
					1973		(see Note)		(see Note)

Note: Some libraries may choose to classify these works following the instruction for Local, A-Z instead of using the collective biography number.

EXERCISE 5.7

a.	R	b.	R	c.	LC	d.	LC	e.	LC
	204		334		1977		2289		577
	.L4		.H6		.G66		.B8		.C55
	1986		.J64		1992		.C96		1997
			1984				1995		

f.	HS	g.	HS	h.	HV	i.	HV
	2189		2230		7269		7270
	.S2		.A8		.B3		.A73
	.S28		.P47		.B76		.R44
	1996		1989		1993		1983

EXERCISE 5.8

a.   HD4300.67
b.   HD4316-4320
c.   HD4295.6
d.   HD4346.5
e.   HD4300.5
f.   HD4284
g.   HD4160.5
h.   HD4056-4060
i.   HD4096-4100
j.   HD4131-4135
k.   HD4236-4240
l.   HD4275.5
m.   HD4415.5
n.   HD4369.3

EXERCISE 5.9

a.   HD4005
b.   HD4165
c.   HD4177.5
d.   HD4147
e.   HD4168
f.   HD4171
g.   HD4150.B7
h.   HD4170.M6
i.   HD4180.D7
j.   HD4010.S2

EXERCISE 5.10

a. HD	b. HD	c. HD	d. HD	e. HD
4147	4168	4005	4177	4010
.D39	.B45	.J46	.5	.Q3
1987	1991	1983	.M47	.R53
			1986	1993

f.   HD
4150
.S3
.F47
1996

EXERCISE 5.11

a. HD	b. HD	c. HD	d. HD	e. HD
4318	4293	4373	4123	4303
.M66	.C53	.Y68	.J33	.K43
1985	1969	1995	1992	1998

EXERCISE 5.12

a. HD
    4135
    .C3
    .S55
    1987

b. HD
    4375
    .S9
    .M67
    1993

c. HD
    4255
    .Z8
    .R64
    1991

d. HD
    4250
    .L5
    .V54
    1996

e. HD
    4310
    .M3
    .Z67
    1989

EXERCISE 5.13

a. HD
    4215
    .7
    .L37
    1992

b. HD
    4170
    .5
    .M87
    1989

c. HD
    4275
    .5
    .S65
    1995

d. HD
    4053
    .L56
    1981

e. HD
    4285
    .9
    .Z8
    .K35
    1998

f. HD
    4300
    .5
    .Z8
    .H36
    1996

g. HD
    4366
    .Z8
    .K83
    1990

h. HD
    4415
    .5
    .Z8
    .A95
    1987

EXERCISE 5.14

a. SF
    624
    .N8
    .T39
    1993

b. SF
    688
    .B3
    .S26
    1986

c. LA
    1462
    .B37
    1981

d. NA
    7469
    .B69
    1993

e. NA
    7471
    .W3
    .J64
    1989

f. HN
    490
    .M3
    .R66
    1983

g. HN
    533
    .5
    .T73
    1978

h. HV
    4840
    .A6
    .S67
    1997

i. B
    2798
    .F83
    1996

EXERCISE 5.15

a. QC
    16
    .E5
    .F65
    1997

b. QC
    16
    .E5
    .A4
    1996

c. P
    92
    .5
    .O54
    .M43
    1991

d. PN
    1998
    .3
    .B47
    .A3
    1988

e. E
    467
    .1
    .E47
    .R36
    1960

f. CT
    144
    .S85
    1991

g. CT
    225
    .C35
    1994

h. HB
    117
    .A3
    .S67
    1990

i. GV
    865
    .A1
    .G75
    1998

j. GV
    850
    .C73
    .A3
    1997

k.   QE
     707
     .T4
     .F38
     1991

Note: The biographee cutter may have one or two digits depending on your shelflist. If you only used one digit in your cutter number, this is not incorrect.

EXERCISE 5.16

a.   BF   b.   BF   c.   B   d.   QA   e.   QL
     723   1779   1611   76   672
     .C3   .F4   .S472   .758   .2
     .P5316   .R6715   .G47   .C6314   .H5817
     1986   1995   1850   1993   1985

f.   PQ   g.   PQ
     6329   6330
     .A3   .A3
     1955   1935

EXERCISE 5.17

a.   Tables P-PZ1 to P-PZ16 are tables for languages and P-PZ20 to P-PZ50 are tables for literature.
b.   Table III
c.   24.8
d.   XL because Cynthia Freeman has a cutter number. Table XXXIX would be used if she was a one-number author.
e.   The cutter number is determined by the second letter of the author's surname.
f.   .A19 followed by date
g.   .Z5A5-Z
h.   By title .xZ46-479

EXERCISE 5.18

a.   PS   b.   PS   c.   PS   d.   PS   e.   PS
     3549   3549   3549   3549   3549
     .U47   .U47   .U47   .U47   .U47
     .Z97   .Z88   .A15   .A6   .A16
     1997   1994   1990   1991   1981

EXERCISE 5.19

a.   PR   b.   PR   c.   PS   d.   PR   e.   PS
     6045   6025   3327   9375   3543
     .O72   .I88   .S95   .9   .I26
     .Z469   .Z49   .H39   .I86   .Z54
     1997   1996   1951   .S54   1997
     (Note 1)   (Note 2)   1990
                                                       (Note 3)

f.	PR	g.	PR	h.	PR	i.	PS	j.	PS
	4483		4061		9619		3275		3550
	.A33		.A2		.3		.G74		.A1
	1987		.A43		.F68		1988		.P75
			1992		.M9		(Note 5)		1996
					1902				
					(Note 4)				

k.	PS	l.	PR
	3550		9639
	.A1		.3
	.O5		.F73
	1997		.Z46
	(Note 6)		1991
			(Note 7)

Note 1: The instructions are to cutter by title so .Z469 represents the letter "m" for memoirs. "M" is in the middle of the alphabet and 469 is in the middle of the range 46-479.

Note 2: The cutter number according to the LC Cutter Table would be .I84. This number fits in to the author cutter numbers already in the schedule. However, your library may prefer that you check the Library of Congress catalog for cutter numbers for literary authors. If you do this for Mitford, you will find that her cutter number is .I88. The .Z49 is cuttered for the correspondent, Waugh.

Note 3: The country is subarranged by Table XXV and that table sends you to Table XL for individual authors or works. So cutter for Ismail as author and then follow the instructions for "Separate works. By title".

Note 4: Table Da (PR) directs you to Table XXI. Individual authors are subarranged by Table XL.

Note 5: The range of numbers for Whittier starts with PS3250 so use the second column of Table XXXI.

Note 6: The number and table for "Anonymous works" is used in this case. The answer assumes that this is American Literature 1961-.

Note 7: Table Da (PR) refers you to Table XXI. Follow the instructions at Biography. Individual. Look for the numbers 196+ and 19+ on the pages that follow in Tables XX and XXI and use the Table XXI instructions.

EXERCISE 6.1

QA	QA	QA	QA	QA	QA
16	16	16	16	39	39
.D58	.G24	.M53	.M533	.S65	.S65
1979	1986	1996	1994	1987	1990

QA	QA	QA	QA	QA	QA
39	39	77	77	77	77
.S652	.S66	.B76	.B766	.F75	.F75
1989	1988	1994	1978	1983	1989

QA	QA	QA
95	95	95
.A33	.A3312	.A332
1986	1991	1975

EXERCISE 6.2

N	N	N	N	N	N
7431	7431	7431	7431	7431	7431
.P47	.Q56	.Q562	.Q563	.5	.5
1973	1990	1974	1989	.A34	.A34
				1986	1990

N	N	N	N	N	N
7431	7432	7432	7432	7432	7432
.5	.I86	.3	.3	.5	.5
.A34	1991	.C64	.D76	.A2	.A78
1996		1991	1995	.J86	.K93
				1994	1982

EXERCISE 6.3

BF	BF	BF	BF	BF	BF
175	175	175	175	175	175
.5	.5	.5	.5	.5	.5
.A72	.D44	.D44	.D74	.D74	.E35
.P43	.C66	.Q36	.W45	.W45	.B53
1989	1993	1993	1990	1994	1993

BF	BF	BF	BF
175	175	175	175
.5	.5	.5	.5
.I43	.K45	.M37	.M37
.P76	.K87	.F76	.F76
1987	1995	1994	1996

EXERCISE 6.4

B831	B831	BD431	BD431	BD431
.2	.2	.K58	.L43	.M897
.N38	.N66	1991	1992	1952
1997	1993			

BF109 .J8M34 1996	BF109 .J8N65 1994	BF109 .J8S74 1994	BF1040 .B25 1993	BF1040 .B255 1992
BF1040 .B35 1990	BH301 .M54F75 1985	BH301 .M54P67 1985	BH301 .M54P67 1988	

EXERCISE 7.1

a. 12
b. 11
c. 0
d. 50
e. 6
f. 19
g. 22

EXERCISE 7.2

a. HD5309
b. HD7255.5
c. HD4928.A5
d. HD6053.5 and HD6053.6.A-Z
e. HD59.2

EXERCISE 7.3

a. HF294
b. Exports
c. You can cutter by region or country for general works and for local areas.
d. 7 captions
   HF5473.A2-Z Latin America
   HF5473.A3-Z By region or country, A-Z

EXERCISE 7.4

a. Higher commercial education
b. International commodity control
c. With the Atlantic
d. Job descriptions. Occupational descriptions
e. Environmental aspects. Green marketing
f. HF5415.I26
g. HF5415.52
h. HF5720

EXERCISE 7.5

a.   8
b.   HD9502.5.A43-A434
c.   97
d.   HD4831
e.   General trade unions, A-Z

EXERCISE 7.6

a.   HD4482
b.   HD5111.A3
c.   HD5110.5
d.   HD2365
e.   HD2336.2

EXERCISE 7.7

a.   Other regions or countries (Table H9)
b.   Table H9
c.   HD4000
d.   HD4342
e.   HD
    4342
    .Z8
    .T863
    1999

Note: Did you remember to expand the second cutter for the main entry?

EXERCISE 8.1

a.	KJ	b.	KJE	c.	KJA	d.	KJE	e.	KKV
	158		542		2270		580		4986
	.M37		.B46		.A63		.E97		.4
	.F47		1979		1955		1990		.C57
	1961								1989

EXERCISE 8.2

a.	K	b.	K	c.	K	d.	K	e.	K
	103		247		670		5293		5301
	.T3		.A3		.A58		.E27		.L39
	.B63		.I58		.Z56		1994		1997
	1989		1985		1981				

f.	K	g.	K
	7340		5087
	.C67		.S4
	1996		.U55
			1994

EXERCISE 8.3

a.   NA701-1614
b.   Table N5 modified
c.   NA700
d.   Special architects, families and firms
e.   NA759.A-Z
f.   NB201-1114
g.   NC101-377
h.   Throughout the schedule
i.   It designates the artist, i.e., either the architect, sculptor, furniture designer, etc.
j.   Yes
k.   No. Most artists will not appear in the index. You will need to use the subclass for a particular media and then the instructions for "Special countries" based on the artist's nationality.

EXERCISE 8.4

a. NC	b. ND	c. NA	d. NA	e. NB
139	237	737	997	497
.P65	.P65	.W75	.E39	.M66
.P43	.A83	.P44	.R69	.A3
1997	1998	1993	1989	1987
(Note 1)	(Note 2)			

f. NK	g. NA	h. NA	i. ND
2635	1455	1605	3159
.F53	.F53	.M87	.A44
.A259	.A256	.B66	1977
1985	1993	1985	
(Note 3)	(Note 4)		

Note 1: These are the sketches of Jackson Pollock so the subclass NC applies. Table N6 has been used.

Note 2: The painting subclass ND applies. The instruction for subarrangement in Table N6 is for the cutter to start after .A8.

Note 3: The instructions in the schedules for "Cutter-number countries" apply.

Note 4: You should apply the table within Table N5 at 755.A-Z.

EXERCISE 8.5

a. HD	b. HD	c. HD	d. SB	e. SK
8039	9529	9710	466	287
.B872	.S623	.U64	.I43	.G72
.U66	.P587	.G463	.G375	.K467
1991	1982	1967	1970	1972

EXERCISE 8.6

a.	HN	b.	HN	c.	HJ	d.	HJ	e.	HV
	530		789		9377		6909		6439
	.Z9		.A85		.6		.R57		.C22
	.E43		.T85		.A4		1998		.O65
	1978		1968		.M37				1976
					1993				

f.	HG	g.	HD	h.	HX	i.	HX	j.	HV
	6242		1122		240		289		9800
	.6		.Z63		.7		.7		.55
	.A2		.M43		.A6		.G73		.Z8
	.M83		1982		.S36		.H65		.B365
	1990				1993		1992		1995

EXERCISE 8.7

a.	HD	b.	HD	c.	HB	d.	HB	e.	HB
	5365		5331		3717		3717		3717
	.M6152		.M72		1929		1929		1857
	1984		1906		.B54		.S73		.A37
	.S29		.M49		1998		1996		1986
	1990		1980						

f.	HB	g.	GV	h.	GV	i.	GV
	3717		722		722		722
	1873		1984		1936		2000
	.S28		.O49		.M36		.S93
	1969		1984		1987		1999

EXERCISE 8.8

a. GV722 1936.M36 1987
b. GV722 1984.O49 1984
c. GV722 2000.S93 1999
d. HB3717 1857.A37 1986
e. HB3717 1873.S28 1969
f. HB3717 1929.B54 1998
g. HB3717 1929.S73 1996
h. HD5331.M72 1906.M49 1980
i. HD5365.M6152 1984.S29 1990

EXERCISE 8.9

a. HD58.8.C65 1988
b. HD58.8.C66 1990
c. HD58.8.D86 1990
d. HD58.8.H36 1989
e. HD58.8.H363 1994
f. HD58.8.H364 1990
g. HD58.8.H365 1988 (Note 1)
h. HD58.8.M32513 1993 (Note 2)

i.   HD58.82.M36 1999
j.   ND1495.P8.G3713 1993 (Note 2)
k.   PR6043.O78.G39818 1983 (Note 2)
l.   TR146.M62 1982
m. TR653.R46313 1998
n.   TR681.F3.K37 1996

Note 1: The answer could also be .H37 and this would leave more space for other works by C. Hardy.

Note 2: This is a translation indicated by **13** or **18** at the end of the cutter. If you remove it, the language of translation will no longer be indicated in the call number. Some libraries may decide that this level of detail is not necessary in their call numbers.

GLOSSARY

abridged edition A condensed form of a work

add In LCC, mathematically adding a number to a base number, e.g., 4000 + 375 = 4375

alphanumeric A combination of letters and numbers

alternate classification number Number provided in a MARC record for other libraries as an alternative to the number used by the Library of Congress for its own collection

append To attach a number to the end of a cutter number

"apply table at" note A note that refers you to another table in the schedule

author The person chiefly responsible for the intellectual or artistic content of a work, e.g., writer of a book, compiler of a bibliography, composer of a musical work, artist, photographer

author number *See* book number

autobiography The story of a person's life written by him/herself

base number The number in the schedules to which a number is added from a table

bibliographic record A description of an item in card, microtext, machine-readable, or other form containing sufficient information to identify the item. It may include subject headings and a call number

bibliography A list of related materials or resources, usually subject-related

biographee A person who is the subject of a biography

biography 1. A written account of a person's life. 2. The branch of literature concerned with people's individual lives

Biography Table Table that can be applied across all schedules to enable subarrangement for individual biography (except when there are specific instructions)

book number The numbers, letters, or combination of numbers and letters used to distinguish an individual item from other items with the same classification number

call number A combination of letters and numbers on a library item consisting of a class number, a book number, and sometimes a location symbol

caption A name, word, or phrase used to name a class number

catalog A list of library materials contained in a collection, a library, or a group of libraries, arranged according to some definite plan

cataloging The preparation of bibliographic information for catalog records. Cataloging consists of descriptive cataloging, subject cataloging, and classification

cataloging-in-publication (CIP) Cataloging data produced by the national library or other agency of the country of publication, included in the work when it is published

Cf. *See* confer note

CIP *See* cataloging-in-publication

class A discipline or subgroup of that discipline represented by a letter or letters, e.g., Q for Science, QA for Mathematics

class number Letters and numbers assigned from the LC schedules to indicate a subject for a given work

classification A system for arranging library materials according to subject

classification number Letters and numbers allocated to a library item to indicate its subject

Classification Plus The electronic version of the Library of Congress classification schedules. Also includes LCSH

classification policy A set of decisions and guidelines developed by a library for classifying materials

classification schedules The set of volumes that make up LCC

classification scheme A particular scheme for arranging library materials according to subject, e.g., Library of Congress Classification, Dewey Decimal Classification

classify To allocate a classification number

collective biography Stories of the lives of a number of people

Colon Classification A classification scheme devised by S. R. Ranganathan for Indian libraries, using numbers and letters, and a colon to separate different parts of the classification number

confer note (Cf.) A note in the LCC schedules that refers you to related class numbers elsewhere in the schedules

copy cataloging Copying cataloging details from an existing catalog record, and adding local location and holdings details

copyright date The date identified in a work by the symbol ©

corporate author An organization or group of people identified by a particular name, and acting as an entity

cutter number A system of author numbers, devised by Charles Ammi Cutter, beginning with the first letter of the author's name and followed by numbers. Used in LCC for authors, titles, geographic areas, and topics

Cutter-Sanborn Table An extension of Cutter's two-figure table expanded and later revised by Kate Sanborn to become a three-figure author table. Designed to maintain works with the same classification number in alphabetical order of author

Cutter Table *See* LC Cutter Table

date of publication The earliest year in which the particular edition of the work was published, e.g., if a second edition was published in 1991, and reprinted without alteration in 1993, the date of publication of this edition is 1991

DDC *See* Dewey Decimal Classification

decimal extension The decimal number that is provided in the schedules as part of a class number to subdivide a topic further

decimal number A number preceded by a decimal point

Dewey Decimal Classification (DDC) A classification scheme devised by Melvil Dewey in 1873, using numbers to represent subjects

delimiter 1. A symbol used to introduce a new subfield in a MARC record. 2. A symbol indicating the end of a set of data in a MARC record, e.g., a record, field, or subfield

discipline A very broad group of subjects in a classification scheme, e.g., music

double cuttering The use of two cutter numbers as part of a call number

editor Person who prepares another person's work for publication

enumerative classification Classification which attempts to spell out (enumerate) all the single and composite subjects required, e.g., Library of Congress Classification

faceted classification Classification which allows for notation to be built up by the use of tables and other parts of the schedules. All modern classification schemes are faceted to a degree. Colon Classification is the definitive faceted classification scheme

facsimile 1. An exact copy. 2. Also fax. Transmission of a document via a telephone line

fiction Prose writing which is the product of the author's imagination

folio 1. The size of a book, usually over 30 cm. Some libraries refer to these as "large" books. 2. A book which is printed on sheets of paper folded once. 3. The individual leaf of a book

foreword A brief statement of the reasons for the book, usually by the author or editor

form 1. The way in which bibliographic text is arranged, e.g., dictionary. 2. Type of literary work, e.g., poetry, drama

heading *See* caption

hierarchical classification Classification in which the division of subjects is from the most general to the most specific, e.g., Dewey Decimal Classification and Library of Congress Classification (to a lesser extent)

hierarchy The ranked order of subjects in a classification scheme

hypertext Information connected via links in the text, with a computer automating movement from one piece of information to another

"including" note A note in the LCC schedules that lists topics included within a subject

incunabula Books printed before 1500

index 1. An alphabetical list of terms or topics in a work, usually found at the back. 2. A systematically arranged list which indicates the contents of a document or group of documents

indentation The use of spacing and formatting to indicate hierarchy in the page layout of the LCC schedules

infobase A collection of information, either text or graphics, that is fully indexed and has functions similar to a database. Used in *Classification Plus*

initial article The word which introduces a noun at the beginning of a title, e.g., the, a, an, le, il, los

Internet A world-wide network of computer networks all linked together

jurisdiction A geographical entity that has the right and power to administer justice and to apply laws

Language and Literature Tables A separate publication for the P schedules that contains all the tables to be used with those schedules

LC *See* Library of Congress

LC Cutter Table A modification of Cutter's original table by the Library of Congress to suit its special needs

LCC *See* Library of Congress Classification

LCSH *See* Library of Congress Subject Headings

Library of Congress The library of the United States Congress; the de facto national library of the United States

Library of Congress Classification A classification scheme developed by the Library of Congress using numbers and letters

Library of Congress Subject Headings The authoritative list of subject headings compiled and maintained by the Library of Congress

literary work A work, other than a sacred work, written in a literary form, e.g., a poem, drama, novel, etc., and regarded as being of high quality

location symbol A symbol showing which collection an item belongs to, e.g., F for fiction

main entry The principal entry in a bibliographic record usually an author or title

main entry cutter The cutter number based on the main entry

MARC Machine readable cataloging. A system developed by the Library of Congress in 1966 so that libraries can share machine readable bibliographic data

memoirs A record of events written from personal observation

mixed notation A combination of types of symbol, e.g., numbers and letters used in Library of Congress Classification. Cf pure notation

notation The series of symbols which stand for the classes, subclasses, divisions and subdivisions of classes

number building Construction of classification numbers not listed in the schedules, following instructions given in the schedules and tables

outline A list at the beginning of each schedule that summarizes the subject content of that schedule

periodical A serial with a distinctive title intended to appear in successive parts at stated and regular intervals. Often used as a synonym for serial

preface The author's or editor's reasons for the book. It appears after the title page and before the introduction

pure notation One type of symbol only, e.g., numbers, used as the notation of a classification scheme. Cf mixed notation

qualifier An addition to a name, etc., enclosed in parentheses

revision A new edition of a schedule that also incorporates changes and additions since the last edition

roman numeral A number like I, II, III, IV, or i, ii, iii, iv, etc.

schedule The enumerated classes of a classification scheme arranged in alphabetical and numerical order

scope note A note in the LCC schedules describing the range and meaning of a class number

"see" note A note in the LCC schedules that refers to a number elsewhere in the schedules

shelflist The record of the works in a library in the order in which they are shelved

shelflisting The process of adjusting a cutter number to fit into the shelflist

subclass A subdivision of a main class, e.g., RA, NK, SB, ZA

subject The theme or themes of a work

subject heading A heading which describes a subject and provides subject access to a catalog

synthetic classification Classification which allows the classifier to construct (synthesize) numbers for composite subjects, e.g., Colon Classification, Universal Decimal Classification

table A set of instructions which appear in table format in the schedules. The use of tables prevents repetition of the same instruction throughout the schedule and enables more specific numbers to be constructed

Translation Table Table that can be applied across all schedules in LCC for subarrangement by language of translation except when there are specific instructions

UDC *See* Universal Decimal Classification

unique call number A number on a library item consisting of a class number, a book number, and often a location symbol, which is different from every other call number in the library

Universal Decimal Classification (UDC) A classification scheme developed by the International Federation for Information and Documentation (FID) by expanding Dewey Decimal Classification. It offers the most specific classification for specialized collections and is widely used in special libraries

Web *See* World Wide Web

website A location on the Internet that houses a set of linked pages or screens

work letter Lower case letter used by the Library of Congress after the date in a LCC number as a method of arranging works on the shelves

World Wide Web A collection of sites on the Internet in which users can move easily from one document or site to another by means of hypertext links

BIBLIOGRAPHY

Chan, Lois Mai. *Immroth's Guide to the Library of Congress Classification,* 4th ed. Englewood, Colo.: Libraries Unlimited, 1990.

The Library of Congress Classification Schedules. Washington, D.C.: Library of Congress, 1948-

Library of Congress Filing Rules. Washington, D.C.: Library of Congress, 1980.

Library of Congress website [online], http://lcweb.loc.gov.

Sayers, W. C. Berwick. *Sayers' Manual of Classification for Librarians*, 5th ed. London: Deutsch, 1975.

Subject Cataloging Manual. Classification. Washington, D.C.: Library of Congress, 1992.

Subject Cataloging Manual. Shelflisting, 2nd ed. Washington, D.C.: Library of Congress, 1995.

INDEX

"apply table at" note, 31
area cutter, 69-70
author number, *See* book number
base number, 93
biography, 67, 102-104
Biography Table, 102-104
book number, 15, 37
call number, 15, 37-73
Cf. *See* confer note
classes, 17
class number, 15, 37
Classification Plus, 121-122
classification policy, 9-10
collective biography, *See* biography
Colon Classification, 8
confer note, 31
corporate author cutter, 62-63
Cutter, Charles Ammi, 11, 42
cutter number, 42-73
Cutter-Sanborn Table, 42
Cutter Table, *See* LC Cutter Table
date
    of conference, 49
    of publication, 48-49
decimal extension, 37-38, 45, 70-72
Dewey Decimal Classification, 8, 11
double cutter, 72-73
enumerative classification, 8, 13
faceted classification, 8
Hanson, James, 11
hierarchical classification, 8
hierarchy, 12
"including" note, 30
incunabula, 10
indentation, 28-29

index, 9, 12, 34
Jefferson, Thomas, 11
Language and Literature Tables, 109-111
LC Cutter Table, 42-45
Library of Congress filing rules, 47
Library of Congress subject headings, 14, 121
location symbol, 15
main entry cutter, 44-45
Martel, Charles, 11
mixed notation, 9
notation, 8-9, 12
notes, 30-31
number building, 9, 13
outline, 25
periodical cutter, 64
pure notation, 9
revision, 9, 13
schedules, 8, 12, 21-31
scope note, 30
see note, 30
shelflisting, 53
shelving, 115-116
shelving cutter, 67-68
spine labeling, 116
subclasses, 19
synthetic classification, 8
tables, 33, 75-111
title cutter, 60-61
topical cutter, 65-66
Translation Table, 106-107
unique call number, 43
Universal Decimal Classification, 8
work letter, 49, 63

ABOUT THE AUTHORS

Helena Dittmann is a librarian at the University of Canberra Library, where she was head of the Cataloging Department for some years. She has trained library staff in all aspects of cataloging and in the use of LCC. She has also tutored in the Library Studies program at the Canberra Institute of Technology, Canberra, Australia.

Jane Hardy is a librarian, library director, teacher and trainer. She has used LCC for many years at the University of Canberra Library and has trained staff in its use. She has been very involved in bibliographic and information technology training at the University. She is currently director of the Curriculum Resources Centre.